HOT LITTLE SUPPERS

HOT LITTLE SUPPERS

Simple Recipes to Feed Family and Friends

CARRIE MOREY

Founder of

HARPER HORIZON

Photography and food styling by Angie Mosier

ISBN 978-0-7852-4162-1 (eBook)
ISBN 978-0-7852-4161-4 (HC)

Library of Congress Control Number: 2021931647

Printed in South Korea

21 22 23 24 25   SAM   10 9 8 7 6 5 4 3 2 1

To John, Caroline, Cate, and Sarah. Thank you for always being hungry and making our supper table my favorite place to be. Thank you also to my bakery family and to my family of customers for all of your support—there is always a place at my table for you!

CONTENTS

INTRODUCTION

Be a Biscuit

Rise tall, be warm and buttery on the inside, and be open to anyone's jam.

Over the last fifteen years of running my handmade biscuit company, Callie's Hot Little Biscuit, and balancing that with being a mom, I've become more convinced of the ways that food can bring people together. Food is my language of love and the way I best communicate with my customers, friends, and family. For me, the heart of our family is sitting down to eat together at the dinner table. It's what keeps us close and sane. It grounds us. No matter what has happened during the day, suppertime is sacred—it heals us all.

Balancing family and work isn't always easy, and the lines sometimes get blurred. My customers and staff are like family, and my family is right there with me in my business. My daughters Caroline and Cate work at Callie's Hot Little Biscuit, and my youngest, Sarah, often pitches in. In the car we are back and forth to games and practices, with some home-work and conference calls thrown in. Throughout their childhoods, the girls have listened in on the inner workings of running a business. They've heard firsthand all of the issues as they arise and all of the problem-solving and brainstorming that follows. They've got-ten an in-depth education. As hectic as it is, I wouldn't have it any other way. I love that my daughters get to see how a business works, and I love how the way I run my business is informed by my family.

No matter how crazy life gets, I always come back to the dinner table and create delicious suppers for and with the girls and my husband, John. On my blog and on Instagram over the years, I've been sharing some of our family favorites, and with *Hot Little Suppers* I'm so excited to give readers tasty ideas for that age-old question: *What am I going to make for supper?* Some are great go-to, on-the-fly weeknight recipes you can whip up between sports practices. Others are what I call weekend recipes, which take a little more time and prep and are perfect for a weekend get-together with friends.

Whether making handmade biscuits with my staff, interacting with my wonderful cus-tomers, or standing next to my daughters and husband in the kitchen, chopping vegetables, the act of making food and showing love is forever intertwined for me. Food is how I express myself, and when it comes to how I try to live my life, raise my children, and run my business, it's no different. Is it any surprise then that my philosophy on life is best described as a biscuit?

Be a biscuit—rise tall, be warm and buttery on the inside, and be open to anyone's jam.

Rise tall. This means to have confidence in yourself, to believe in yourself. Even when I was four years old, my dad would tell me, "Stand up straight. Look people in the eye." Carry yourself in a way that people can see you love yourself and love others. I've learned that you have to love yourself before you can fully love anyone else.

And that's another lesson biscuits can teach us. Biscuits rise taller when they have other biscuits around them. When you put biscuits on a pan to bake, if they're not placed close together, they don't rise as much. They fall to one side or the other. When they're placed close together, they grab on to each other and pull each other up, rising tall and proud.

We as humans do the same thing: we rise tall when we stand together.

Be warm and buttery. This one is simple. Biscuits are warm and buttery. That's why we love them! Lead with kindness and warmth always.

Be open to anyone's jam. The world has as many different kinds of people as delicious fillings and toppings for biscuits. So many different colors, races, and flavors of personality, language, and culture make our world much more fun—I see this in action every day with my staff. I believe strongly that we're equal and should be treated as such. That is one of the most important lessons I hope to emulate for my bakery and home family. I'm proud to see that we're raising our children to truly believe in equality for all and to fight for this in their daily lives. It's a constant necessity, and we must continue to work on it.

As a society we still have far to go, but I do have hope that we'll become better as we open our hearts and minds and embrace one another. If you're confident in yourself and you lead with a kind heart, it's easy to be open because you don't fear what may seem different from you.

One of my favorite ways to experience new people and cultures is through food! Food is how we celebrate with each other and how we commiserate with each other. It unites us on a local and universal level. It helps us heal hurts in our own families and communities, and it fosters love and appreciation for people and cultures all over the planet. I travel every chance I get, and that has become my number one inspiration for my recipes. Combining what I learn from other people and cultures with my own food history is a way of honoring what we all share in common: a craving for flavorful food that nurtures our bodies and spirits.

I'm not an expert on any particular cuisine, but I am a passionate fan of the flavors and methods of every place I get to visit. For me,

learning about someone's culture through food is a way to instantly connect with them. Hearing the story of how someone across the globe makes a certain dish that is similar to one my family makes, such as traditional red rice in Guam and okra and tomatoes in India, reminds me that despite all of our delicious variations, we are all cut from the same cloth. We are more alike than we are different, and our differences, once shared, only make us stronger together.

That is why I love sharing food with people. Sharing food is such an instant connection that breaks down barriers because you immediately have something in common. We all eat, and we all have a story behind our meals that we want to share.

Be confident, be kind, and be open to everybody. If I can continue to raise my children to live by those three maxims, I feel as though they'll be more able to deal with the sticky situations in life. We all have our moments when emotions get the best of us. It takes practice to be a biscuit. I am a work in progress! But I've learned—and it *is* a learned skill—that when we believe in ourselves, when we lead with kindness, and when we accept others, we can find some way through to the other side, and there are bound to be biscuits around us to help us rise to the occasion.

In *Hot Little Suppers*, I hope you'll find lots of opportunities to make, eat, and be a biscuit. It feels so good to share food with the ones we love, to gather around the dinner table, to talk about our day, and to enjoy each other's company. As much as I love cooking and eating, I truly believe that the food itself doesn't always have to be the star. Some nights, supper might be fast food from a drive-through. It might be a rotisserie chicken and a bagged salad. We don't always have the luxury of making a homemade meal. For me, when it comes to the art of sitting down for supper, it's not the food that's most important. What is most important is the ritual of stopping whatever else we're doing, turning off all the electronics, sitting down at the table, and giving our full attention to each other.

Sitting down together at the table as a family is a priority for me. It's sacred ground. What better way to end the day than feeling love for each other? And enjoying good food? It sure does make getting up the next morning and facing what's ahead a whole lot easier.

And if you're like me, I don't finish one meal before I'm thinking about the next one. Supper isn't mere sustenance for me. I live my life looking forward to the next meal, event, or occasion to celebrate life. Making an event out of cooking and eating food makes life more fun.

My hope is that *Hot Little Suppers* offers lots of recipes you'll want to try with and for your family. The book starts with a chapter on biscuits because that's what got us here in the first place and because biscuits are as good for supper as for breakfast! Then, chapters for each season—spring, summer, fall, and winter—include recipes for weeknight suppers, weekend suppers, and what I call "Hot Little Extras." Sometimes, instead of a meal with an entrée and sides, I just want to eat the sides. And other times I'd rather eat a couple of appetizers as a meal. These "extras" are recipes you can eat all on their own or make part of a bigger meal. For each season, I also include a few cocktail and dessert recipes. At the end of the book, you'll find an appendix with my super-easy go-to methods for quick veggie and salad sides all year long, which pair well with almost anything.

To make it even easier for you to figure out which recipe is perfect for any occasion—whether it's a routine weekday meal with your family or a celebration where you'll need to feed a crowd—each entrée is labeled with an icon:

    Crowd Pleaser

    Family Fave

    One-Pot Meal

    Quick Fix

    Vegetarian

    Weeknight or Weekend

Sitting down for supper together as a family and doing our best to be a biscuit doesn't automatically create peace, love, and harmony. It's not a magic wand. But for me, when I practice doing it, I find that it feels pretty magical. Whether we're with family or a group of strangers, having a meal together, sharing that ritual, can break down walls and help us find common ground. Even if we have nothing else in common with each other, we're all nourished by food. I believe it's a powerful starting point. I believe we can solve a lot of the world's problems over a shared meal, sitting around the table together.

We may not be perfect, our suppers may not be perfect, and our biscuits may not be perfect. But when we sit down together with confidence, kindness, and openness, we can better handle all of our own imperfections and all that is broken in this world, because we're surrounded by love and acceptance. And that is something to practice and celebrate every chance we get.

Let's rise tall together!

CARRIE'S GROCERY LIST

With these items, you can make so many meals. I keep a running list to be sure I've always got these on hand.

White Lily flour (unbleached self-rising and all-purpose; this is my preferred brand)

Semolina flour

Cornmeal

Olive oil (I get a big canister because we go through so much of it.)

Sesame oil (toasted)

Canola oil

Vinegars: white, rice wine, red wine, white wine

Mirin

Kosher salt

Peppercorns (I buy these in bulk because they last so long. Then, so I don't have to take time while cooking, I grind the peppercorns in a spice grinder and keep the ground pepper in vessels by the chopping block, on the stove, and in the dining room.)

Spices (I keep my spices in labeled mason jars.)

Sugars: granulated, brown, turbinado, and confectioners (also known as powdered, 10X, and icing sugar)

Full-fat coconut milk

Fish sauce

Hot sauce (I prefer Red Clay brand.)

San Marzano canned tomatoes

Chipotle peppers

Artichoke hearts

Tuna (I keep basic tuna in water for tuna salad and tuna casserole, and fancier tuna in olive oil to serve over pasta for a weeknight meal.)

Canned white beans (I use these to whip up a quick soup or mix with tuna, herbs, onions, and crostini for a weeknight meal.)

Broth/stock (I keep store-bought broth in the pantry, but I also try to have a few quart containers of homemade stock in the freezer—always chicken and beef and sometimes seafood.)

Pasta

Israeli couscous (also called pearl couscous)

Basmati rice

Pine nuts (I keep these in the freezer, so they last longer.)

Sunflower seeds

Pepitas (roasted and salted)

Nuts

Granola

Popcorn (I keep kernels of white or yellow.)

Fridge and Freezer

Salted butter

Eggs (I typically use large.)

Milk

Whole buttermilk

Cheese (I keep sharp Cheddar, Parmesan, Cotija, feta, and blue cheese on hand. My favorite blue cheese is Clemson blue cheese from Clemson University in South Carolina. Also, I save Parmesan rinds for soups and stews.)

Cream cheese

Olives

Pickles (I like Claussen brand.)

Plain yogurt (for breakfast and for dips, sauces, and marinades)

Whole-grain Dijon mustard (for dressings and putting on meats)

Tomato paste

Horseradish (I prepare my own horseradish by peeling the root with my veggie peeler, then mincing with a Microplane.)

Fresh ginger

Frozen fruit (for breakfast smoothies, on yogurt, and for desserts)

Frozen veggies (corn, pearl onions, and peas)

Frozen homemade stock

Versatile meats like whole chicken, chicken thighs, ground beef, ground pork, and strip or skirt steaks (For chicken, I get the butcher to spatchcock whole chickens, removing the backbone, then at home I use the backbones to make chicken stock.)

Bacon

PRODUCE

Onions: red, white, and yellow (I keep these on the counter.)

Green onions (also called scallions)

Garlic

Shallots

Lettuce (romaine, butter, arugula, and mixed greens)

Spinach (I add spinach to almost everything, so there's always a vegetable.)

Lemons and limes by the bag

Carrots

Celery

Avocado

Tomatoes (regular tomatoes as well as cherry and small heirloom)

Jalapeño peppers

Cucumbers (I like Persian.)

Flat-leaf Italian parsley and cilantro (from the store)

Thyme, mint, oregano, and rosemary (from my garden)

Charleston Rice Steamer

CARRIE'S TOOLS

18 x 13-inch rimmed baking sheet ("half sheet pan")

Wire baking/cooling rack to fit baking sheet

Cast-iron skillet

Sauté pan

Dutch oven

Saucepan

Large pot

Rolling pin

Two-inch biscuit cutter

Parchment paper

Large stainless steel bowl

Chef's knife

Paring knife

Chantry knife sharpener

Messermeister vegetable peeler

Microplane zester

Mandoline slicer

Garlic press

Bamboo and wire skimmer

Digital thermometer with probe

Instant-read meat thermometer

Kitchen twine

Wooden skewers

Mason jars in a variety of sizes

Tongs

Whisk

Ladle

Rubber spatula

Spatula

Pastry brush

Hand mixer

Electric stand mixer

Blender (I love Vitamix brand.)

Food processor

Immersion blender

Pie dish

Ramekins

Colander or strainer

Cocktail shaker

Kitchen towels (Tons! I don't use paper towels.)

Aprons

BISCUITS

Biscuits are part of my everyday life. Not only have I built my philosophy of life around them, but I have been able to create the life I want because of biscuits. When I first decided to start a business, I wanted to do something in the cooking world, but I also wanted to balance that with being a mom. Making and selling biscuits became a manageable way (most of the time!) for me to make both of those dreams come true.

As someone who grew up in the South, biscuits were passed down to me from my mother and grandmothers and already in my blood. Biscuits have no economic barriers. They can be sold at a roadside truck stop for fifty-nine cents or served on a silver platter at the finest of cocktail parties. Everyone loves biscuits, and that's something that brings us together. Biscuits are the daily bread of the South, and the possibilities for making, using, and repurposing them are endless. They can be part of a meal, or they can *be* the meal. They can be sweet or savory, soft or crunchy, stuffed with something to make a sandwich or enjoyed on their own. Leftovers can be turned into croutons, bread crumbs, and even biscuit casseroles. Leftover dough can become biscuit bowls, crackers, and the best egg-in-a-hole you've ever tasted. Southerners are known for their resourcefulness, and as a biscuit baker whose wholesale business handcrafts over ten thousand biscuits a day, I'm always looking for creative and delicious ways to stretch biscuit dough as far as it will go.

Think of the Buttermilk Biscuit recipe as a starting point in your own kitchen and the biscuit as a blank canvas. Stuff it, frost it, slather it, sprinkle it with whatever inspires you. Make your own hot little biscuits for hot little suppers and beyond. Even if they don't become your life's work, they're guaranteed to make your family meals a little warmer, a little more buttery on the inside.

BUTTERMILK BISCUITS

MUSHROOM GRAVY

SAVORY THYME BUTTER

CINNAMON BUTTER

CINNAMON BISCUITS

CREAMSICLE BISCUITS

WHIPPING CREAM BISCUITS

BISCUIT BERRY NESTS

BISCUIT DOUGHNUT HOLES

UNEXPECTED CREATIONS FROM
LEFTOVER BISCUITS AND DOUGH

Savory Southern Biscuit Casserole

Toasted Maple Biscuit Casserole

Biscuit Bowls

Biscuit Crackers

Eggs in a Hole

HOT LITTLE TIPS

Biscuits

- In general, I like to read a recipe all the way through ahead of time. That way, I can make sure I have the ingredients and equipment needed, as well as enough time to make it.

- Mix your biscuit dough in a metal bowl with high sides. A large metal bowl has enough room for your hands to get in there and work the dough. It's also lightweight, easy to clean, and ideal for tossing salads or holding a huge pile of movie-night popcorn.

- When you're adding the liquid to the dry ingredients for biscuit dough, don't worry about the exact measurement of liquid so much as paying attention to the texture. You want to add just enough liquid a little at a time so that the dough is "wetty," tacky, and sticky—wet and messy but not sloppy.

- After two roll-outs of biscuit dough, the dough becomes too tough to use for more biscuits. However, that doesn't mean you have to throw the dough away. Use it to make Biscuit Bowls (page 29), Biscuit Crackers (page 31), Eggs in a Hole (page 33), or get creative and experiment. If you're making biscuits and the biscuits don't fill the pan, you can roll the leftover dough into a snake and nestle it next to the biscuits on the pan, so they have a friend to help them rise. Then, when the biscuits are finished baking, you have an edible reward you can snack on that doesn't take away from your stock of fresh biscuits.

- If you have leftover biscuits, you can use them to make Savory Southern Biscuit Casserole (page 26), chop them up to make croutons, or pop them in the food processor and make bread crumbs.

- You can also freeze leftover biscuits. Wrap the biscuits in foil. Bake from frozen in a 400-degree oven for 25 to 30 minutes. Open the top of the foil for the last 3 to 5 minutes to brown them a little on top. Pro tip: Defrost your biscuits on the countertop to cut the baking time in half.

BUTTERMILK BISCUITS

I believe it's important to remember where you came from. Without this Buttermilk Biscuit recipe, I wouldn't be where I am today. It's the original little biscuit recipe, the one and only, the one my mother, Callie, taught me. I built my whole business around this recipe, and I love being able to share it.

Makes 10 to 12 (2-inch) biscuits

2 ½ cups self-rising flour, ½ cup reserved for dusting

6 tablespoons butter (4 tablespoons cut into small cubes, at room temperature, and 2 tablespoons melted)

¼ cup cream cheese, cut into cubes, at room temperature

¾ to 1 cup whole buttermilk (may substitute low-fat buttermilk)

1. Preheat the oven to 450 degrees. Make sure the oven rack is in the middle position.

2. In a large bowl, combine 2 cups of the flour and the 4 tablespoons of cubed butter. Incorporate the butter into the flour, working the dough between your thumb and middle and pointer fingers to "snap" the dough together until the mixture resembles cottage cheese. It will be chunky with some loose flour. Add the cream cheese and mix it into the flour with your fingers, leaving a few larger pieces.

3. Make a well in the center of your flour mixture. Pour in the buttermilk a little bit at a time, using your hands or a small rubber spatula to mix the flour into the buttermilk until the texture is "wetty," tacky, and sticky. You may not need all of the buttermilk, or you may even need to use a little more. You want the dough to be wet and messy but not sloppy.

4. Sprinkle flour on top of the dough. Run a rubber spatula around the inside of the bowl, creating a separation between the dough and the bowl. Sprinkle a bit more flour in this crease.

5. Generously flour a work surface or flexible baking mat. With force, dump the dough from the bowl onto the surface. Flour the top of the dough and the rolling pin. Roll out the dough into an oval shape 2 inches thick. (No kneading is necessary—the less you mess with the dough, the better.)

6. Flour a 2-inch biscuit cutter. Start from the edge of the rolled-out dough and cut straight through the dough with the cutter, trying to maximize the number of biscuits cut from this first roll-out.

7. Roll out the excess dough after the first biscuits are cut, and cut more biscuits. As long as the dough stays wet inside, you can use as much flour on the outside as you need to handle the dough.

8. Place the biscuits on a rimmed baking sheet lined with parchment paper with

the biscuit sides touching. (It doesn't matter what size pan you use as long as it has a lip or sides and the biscuits are touching.)

9. Brush the tops with the 2 tablespoons of melted butter.

10. Bake for 16 to 18 minutes, or until the biscuit tops are golden brown, rotating the pan halfway through the baking time.

MUSHROOM GRAVY

I have served biscuits with this gravy for a Sunday supper for the five of us, and I have served it at events for hundreds of people. The reaction is always the same: so delicious! Biscuits and gravy has never tasted more sophisticated.

Makes 8 servings (4 cups total)

2 tablespoons olive oil

1 onion, diced, skins reserved for stock (about 1 cup)

2 cloves garlic, minced, skins reserved for stock (about 2 teaspoons)

1 pound mushrooms, cleaned and chopped with stems removed and reserved for stock

4 tablespoons butter

4 tablespoons all-purpose flour

Mushroom stock (see below)

2 tablespoons chopped fresh thyme

2 tablespoons chopped fresh parsley

Salt and pepper to taste

1/2 cup crème fraîche

MUSHROOM STOCK

Reserved mushroom stems

Reserved skins of onion

Reserved skins of garlic cloves

1 bundle fresh thyme (12 stems)

1 bundle fresh parsley (12 stems)

4 cups water

1. To make the mushroom stock: In a medium saucepan, combine mushroom stems, onion and garlic skins, thyme, parsley, and water. Simmer over low heat for 1 hour.

2. Strain the stock over a large bowl. Discard the solids from the strainer. You should have about 2 cups of stock in the bowl. Set aside.

3. Heat the olive oil in a 12-inch skillet over medium heat. Add the onions and garlic and sauté until onions are tender and translucent, about 6 to 8 minutes. Add the mushrooms and sauté until the moisture has cooked off, about 10 to 12 minutes. The mushroom slices will separate from each other and darken in color.

4. Add the butter to the skillet and stir until melted.

5. Add the flour and stir until everything is evenly coated. Slowly add the mushroom stock, stirring constantly until the mixture is smooth and velvety. Add the thyme, parsley, and salt and pepper. Reduce the heat to low and simmer for 30 to 45 minutes, stirring frequently.

6. Add the crème fraîche and stir to combine. Simmer on low another 10 minutes, stirring frequently. Remove from the heat, taste for salt and pepper, and serve immediately over buttermilk biscuits.

Note: I like to use local oyster mushrooms, but you can use whichever kind you prefer.

SAVORY THYME BUTTER

This spread is in my first cookbook, but I had to include it again. It is so versatile—you can put it on fish, roasted chicken, or seared steak. It enhances the flavor of everything it touches, making simple dishes sing. My freezer is never without it.

Makes about 2/3 cup

8 tablespoons (1 stick) butter, at room temperature

1 clove garlic, minced (about 1 teaspoon)

2 tablespoons minced green onion (1 onion, white and green parts)

1 teaspoon minced fresh thyme, or more to taste

Kosher salt and freshly ground black pepper (more than you think you'll need)

HOT LITTLE TIP

This freezes well and is always on my turkey-day table. It's also great with fish, chicken, or steak!

1. In a medium bowl, combine the butter, garlic, green onions, thyme, and a generous amount of salt and pepper to taste with a rubber spatula or whip with a hand mixer.

2. Transfer to a ramekin, cover with plastic wrap, and store in the fridge, or roll into a log on plastic wrap and freeze for up to five months until ready to use.

CINNAMON BUTTER

Cinnamon butter is famous at Callie's Hot Little Biscuit, and we put packets of it in the frozen biscuits we sell online and in grocery stores. Get creative and use this on anything that could use a healthy dose of sweet, buttery decadence.

Makes about 2/3 cup

8 tablespoons (1 stick) butter, at room temperature

1 teaspoon ground cinnamon

1 tablespoon firmly packed light brown sugar

1 1/2 tablespoons white sugar

1. In a medium bowl, combine the butter, cinnamon, brown sugar, and white sugar with a rubber spatula or whip with a hand mixer.

2. Transfer to a ramekin, cover with plastic wrap, and store in the fridge, or roll into a log on plastic wrap and freeze for up to five months until ready to use.

CINNAMON BISCUITS

These are the most popular biscuits at Callie's Hot Little Biscuit, and for good reason! The inspiration for these biscuits is that sweet childhood memory of making cinnamon toast. At home, we keep a huge mason jar of premixed cinnamon sugar on the counter, and the girls make cinnamon toast several times a week. Customers have told us that these cinnamon biscuits have become a Christmas morning tradition for their families, and I feel so honored by that. If you have any leftovers (doubtful!), you can use them to make Toasted Maple Biscuit Casserole (page 27).

Makes 10 to 12 (2-inch) biscuits

2 ½ cups self-rising flour, ½ cup reserved for dusting

6 tablespoons salted butter (4 tablespoons cut into small cubes, at room temperature, and 2 tablespoons melted)

¼ cup cream cheese, cut into cubes, at room temperature

1 tablespoon white sugar

1 tablespoon firmly packed brown sugar

¼ tablespoon ground cinnamon

¾ to 1 cup whole buttermilk

Turbinado sugar for sprinkling

Cinnamon butter (page 9)

Cinnamon Topping

¾ cup white sugar

¾ cup firmly packed light brown sugar

6 tablespoons ground cinnamon

1. Preheat the oven to 350 degrees. Make sure the oven rack is in the middle position.

2. To make the cinnamon topping: In a small bowl, combine the white sugar, brown sugar, and cinnamon. Set aside. You will not need all of the topping for this recipe. You can save what's left and use it to top almost anything, from toast to biscuit doughnut holes.

3. In a large bowl, combine 2 cups of the flour and the 4 tablespoons of cubed butter. Incorporate the butter into the flour, working the dough between your thumb and middle and pointer fingers to "snap" the dough together, until the mixture resembles cottage cheese. It will be chunky with some loose flour.

4. Add the cream cheese and mix it into the flour with your fingers, leaving a few larger pieces.

5. Add the white sugar, brown sugar, and cinnamon. Stir to combine.

6. Make a well in the center of the flour mixture. Pour in the buttermilk a little bit at a time, using your hands or a small rubber spatula to mix the flour into the buttermilk until the texture is "wetty," tacky, and sticky. You may not need all of the buttermilk, or you may even need

to use a little more. You want the dough to be wet and messy but not sloppy.

7. Sprinkle flour on top of the dough. Run a rubber spatula around the inside of the bowl, creating a separation between the dough and the bowl. Sprinkle a bit more flour in this crease.

8. Generously flour a work surface or flexible baking mat. With force, dump the dough from the bowl onto the surface. Flour the top of the dough and the rolling pin. Roll out the dough into an oval shape 2 inches thick.

9. Flour a 2-inch biscuit cutter. Start from the edge of the rolled-out dough and cut straight through the dough with the cutter, trying to maximize the number of biscuits cut from this first roll-out.

10. Roll out the excess dough after the first biscuits are cut, and cut more biscuits. As long as the dough stays wet inside,

you can use as much flour on the outside as you need to handle the dough.

11. Place the biscuits on a rimmed baking sheet lined with parchment paper with the biscuit sides touching. (It doesn't matter what size pan you use as long as it has a lip or sides and the biscuits are touching.)

12. Brush the tops with the 2 tablespoons of melted butter. Sprinkle with cinnamon topping and turbinado sugar, about 1 teaspoon of each per biscuit.

13. Bake for 16 to 18 minutes, or until the biscuit tops are golden brown, rotating the pan halfway through the baking time.

14. Sprinkle a little more turbinado sugar on the biscuits, then let them cool slightly. Split the biscuits in half and spread with cinnamon butter. Serve warm.

HOT
LITTLE
STORY

During the book tour for my first cookbook, people would always ask, "Where can we get your little biscuits hot?" They wanted to be able to walk in somewhere and get a fresh, hot biscuit. I kept replaying the question in my mind: *Where can they get hot little biscuits?* I wondered if we could have a biscuit outpost. Rather than a revenue stream, I envisioned it solely as a way to promote the online and wholesale biscuit business. I based the business plan on how many customers I needed so I wouldn't lose money. I found a bare-bones space, an alley really, that was eight feet wide and eighty feet deep. It wasn't long before I realized the name of the new outpost had been there all along: Hot Little Biscuit. I never would have guessed that this grab-and-go eatery would blossom into three more locations, a food truck, a catering business, and a following all its own. I love the way Callie's Hot Little Biscuit has allowed me to connect with customers, experiment with flavors, get feedback, collaborate with employees, and share all the wonderful blessings that come with being a biscuit.

CREAMSICLE BISCUITS

When we opened the Callie's Hot Little Biscuit in Charlotte, North Carolina, an employee and I were talking about the importance of biscuits in our lives. He told me about his grandmother, who made banana pudding biscuits and creamsicle biscuits. That idea of creamsicle biscuits stayed with me, reminding me of childhood days when I waited for the ice cream truck so I could get an orange push pop.

When I was paired with my dear friend Cheryl Day (a badass in all things baking) from Back in the Day Bakery for a collaboration at the Charleston Wine + Food festival, I finally had the chance to build the creamsicle biscuit of my dreams. I came up with the biscuit part, and Cheryl created the frosting. We decorated the biscuits with edible flowers and a sprinkle of turbinado sugar. Five to six hundred people attended the event, and the line at our food truck was thirty to forty feet deep. We couldn't keep up. It was a three-hour event, and we sold out in the first hour. These biscuits are worth standing in line for. The good news is, you don't have to!

Makes 10 to 12 (2-inch) biscuits

2 ½ cups self-rising flour, ½ cup reserved for dusting

10 tablespoons butter (8 tablespoons cut into small cubes, at room temperature, and 2 tablespoons melted)

⅓ cup white sugar

⅓ cup firmly packed brown sugar

Zest of 1 orange (about 1 to 1 ½ tablespoons)

½ cup whole milk

¼ cup orange juice

1 teaspoon vanilla extract

3 tablespoons turbinado sugar

CHERYL'S FROSTING

5 tablespoons salted butter, at room temperature

1 (8-ounce) package cream cheese, cut into cubes, at room temperature

1 teaspoon vanilla extract

Zest and juice of 2 oranges, divided (about 2 to 2 ½ tablespoons zest and ½ cup juice)

Pinch of salt

2 to 3 cups powdered sugar

GARNISH

3 tablespoons turbinado sugar

1 tablespoon orange zest

1. Preheat the oven to 400 degrees. Make sure the oven rack is in the middle position.

2. In a large bowl, combine 2 cups of the flour and the 8 tablespoons of cubed butter. Incorporate the butter into the flour, working the dough between your

thumb and middle and pointer fingers to "snap" the dough together, until the mixture resembles cottage cheese. It will be chunky with some loose flour.

3. Add the white sugar, brown sugar, and orange zest. Stir to combine.

4. In a small bowl, combine the milk, orange juice, and vanilla. Whisk to combine.

5. Make a well in the center of the flour mixture. Pour in the milk mixture a little bit at a time, using your hands or a small rubber spatula to mix the flour into the milk mixture until the texture is "wetty," tacky, and sticky. You may not need all of the milk mixture. You want the dough to be wet and messy but not sloppy.

6. Sprinkle flour on top of the dough. Run a rubber spatula around the inside of the bowl, creating a separation between the dough and the bowl. Sprinkle a bit more flour in this crease.

7. Generously flour a work surface or flexible baking mat. With force, dump the dough from the bowl onto the surface. Flour the top of the dough and the rolling pin. Roll out the dough into an oval shape 1 1/2 inches thick.

8. Flour a 2-inch biscuit cutter. Start from the edge of the rolled-out dough and cut straight through the dough with the cutter, trying to maximize the number of biscuits cut from this first roll-out.

9. Roll out the excess dough after the first biscuits are cut, and cut more biscuits. As long as the dough stays wet inside, you can use as much flour on the outside as you need to handle the dough.

10. Place the biscuits on a rimmed baking sheet lined with parchment paper with the biscuit sides touching. (It doesn't matter what size pan you use as long as it has a lip or sides and the biscuits are touching.)

11. Brush the tops with the 2 tablespoons of melted butter and sprinkle with turbinado sugar.

12. Bake for 14 to 16 minutes, or until the biscuit tops are golden brown, rotating the pan halfway through the baking time.

13. Remove the biscuits from the oven and let them cool completely.

14. To make the frosting: In the bowl of a stand mixer fitted with the paddle attachment (or in a large mixing bowl using a hand mixer), combine the butter, cream cheese, vanilla, zest, and salt until smooth and creamy, about 3 to 5 minutes. Gradually add the powdered sugar, beating until super light and fluffy, another 3 to 5 minutes. Slowly add the orange juice until it reaches frosting consistency. You may not need to use all of the orange juice to get your desired consistency. (When using a stand mixer, the frosting is lighter in texture and requires a little less orange juice, about 2 to 4 tablespoons less, than when using a hand mixer. But there's no difference in quality or taste.) If not using immediately, you can refrigerate for up to 5 days and then bring to room temperature and rewhip before serving.

15. To make the garnish: in a small bowl, combine the turbinado sugar and orange zest.

16. Frost each biscuit with the frosting and sprinkle the orange zest mixture on top to garnish.

HOT LITTLE TIP

Avoid a Hot Little Mess

If you've made a lot of biscuits, you're probably used to rolling out the biscuit dough so it's 2 inches thick. This biscuit dough, however, has a higher sugar and butter content, which makes the biscuits rise taller than buttermilk biscuits. It's a mistake you'd only make once because the baking biscuit dough rising up and over the pan and spilling into the oven makes a horrific mess you won't soon forget. Spare yourself the learning experience and be sure to roll this dough out to only 1 $^1/2$ inches before you stamp out the biscuits.

WHIPPING CREAM BISCUITS

My dear friend and mentor Nathalie Dupree first taught me about whipping cream biscuits to show just how simple making biscuits can be. This is my take on her two-ingredient wisdom!

Makes 10 to 12 (2-inch) biscuits

2 ½ cups self-rising flour, ½ cup reserved for dusting

1 cup heavy whipping cream

1. Preheat the oven to 450 degrees. Make sure the oven rack is in the middle position.
2. In a large bowl, place 2 cups of the flour.
3. Slowly add the heavy cream to the flour, mixing until the dough comes together (it will be a tough dough).
4. Sprinkle flour on top of the dough. Run a rubber spatula around the inside of the bowl, creating a separation between the dough and the bowl. Sprinkle a bit more flour in this crease.
5. Generously flour a work surface or flexible baking mat. With force, dump the dough from the bowl onto the surface. Flour the top of the dough and the rolling pin. Roll out the dough into an oval shape 2 inches thick.
6. Flour a 2-inch biscuit cutter. Start from the edge of the rolled-out dough and cut straight through the dough with the cutter, trying to maximize the number of biscuits from this first roll-out.
7. Roll out the excess dough after the first biscuits are cut, and cut more biscuits. Place the biscuits on a rimmed baking sheet lined with parchment paper with the biscuit sides touching. (It doesn't matter what size pan you use as long as it has a lip or sides and the biscuits are touching.)
8. Bake for 16 to 18 minutes, or until the biscuit tops are golden brown, rotating the pan halfway through the baking time.

BISCUIT BERRY NESTS

This dessert uses our shortcake dough, a biscuit dough that's a little sweeter than the buttermilk dough. With this dessert, you get the feel of a cobbler but with a unique presentation, where you can see the beautiful berries nested in a buttery crust. I thought up the concept of biscuit nests when I was trying to figure out what to do with leftover biscuit dough after stamping out biscuits. This is the sweet version. For the savory version, check out Eggs in a Hole (page 33).

Makes 5 to 6 servings

2 1/2 cups self-rising flour, 1/2 cup reserved for dusting

7 tablespoons butter (6 tablespoons cut into small cubes, at room temperature, and 1 tablespoon melted)

1/3 cup plus 2 tablespoons white sugar

Pinch of ground cinnamon

1 teaspoon plus a splash of vanilla extract

1/3 to 1/2 cup whole milk

2 to 3 cups mixed berries

1 tablespoon turbinado sugar

Whipped cream or ice cream to serve, if desired

HOT LITTLE TIP

Thank You Berry Much

A six-ounce package of berries is a little bit more than a cup.

1. Preheat the oven to 400 degrees. Make sure the oven rack is in the middle position.

2. In a large bowl, combine 2 cups of the flour and the 6 tablespoons of cubed butter. Incorporate the butter into the flour, working the dough between your thumb and middle and pointer fingers to "snap" the dough together, until the mixture resembles cottage cheese. It will be chunky with some loose flour.

3. Combine the white sugar and cinnamon. Add to the dough and stir.

4. In a small bowl, whisk together the vanilla and milk.

5. Make a well in the center of the flour mixture. Pour in the milk mixture a little bit at a time, using your hands or a small rubber spatula to mix the flour into the milk mixture until the texture is "wetty," tacky, and sticky. You may not need all of the milk mixture. You want the dough to be wet and messy but not sloppy.

6. Sprinkle flour on top of the dough. Run a rubber spatula around the inside of the bowl, creating a separation between the dough and the bowl. Sprinkle a bit more flour in this crease.

7. Generously flour a piece of parchment paper. With force, dump the dough from the bowl onto the paper. Flour the top of the dough and the rolling pin.

Roll out the dough into a 2-inch thick round.

8. Flour a 2-inch biscuit cutter. Start from the edge of the rolled-out dough and cut straight through the dough, making five or six biscuits, about 2 inches apart.

9. Place the parchment paper with the dough onto a rimmed baking sheet. Remove the cut-out biscuits from the centered dough round and line them up along the edge of the sheet. (It's okay for the biscuits to touch each other.) Fill the holes in the dough with heaping servings of berries.

10. Brush the biscuits and the dough round with the 1 tablespoon of melted butter. Sprinkle all with turbinado sugar.

11. Bake the berry-filled dough and biscuits for 16 to 18 minutes, until the biscuit tops are golden brown, rotating the pan halfway through the baking time.

12. To serve, slice the berry-filled round into pie-like wedges. Top each slice with whipped cream or ice cream, if desired. You can serve each portion with a biscuit or save the cut-out biscuits for later.

Note: For the mixed berries, I recommend strawberries, raspberries, blueberries, and blackberries.

BISCUIT DOUGHNUT HOLES

My girls love to make sweets. It's all they think about! One night, we were having a Greek-themed meal for a Sunday supper, when Cate asked about dessert—much more interesting to her than what we were having for supper. *Hmm, what could go with Greek food?* While I was cooking, I told Cate how to make whipping cream biscuit dough, add a bit of sugar and vanilla, and roll the dough into balls. We fried them in a little oil, then kept them warm in the oven while we ate our meal. After supper, we took them out of the oven, drizzled them with honey, and sprinkled on crushed pistachios. I thought they were delicious. The girls ate a few—then immediately rolled the rest in cinnamon sugar. Feel free to experiment with toppings on these easy sweet bites, including cinnamon sugar or powdered sugar.

Makes about 4 to 6 servings (24 biscuit doughnut holes)

3 cups canola oil

2 cups self-rising flour

1/3 cup sugar

1 cup heavy whipping
cream

2 teaspoons vanilla extract

Honey

Crushed pistachios

1. Line a cooling rack with paper towels.

2. Preheat the oil in a small saucepan to 350 degrees. Keep an eye on the temperature the entire time, not letting it get over 350 degrees.

3. In a large bowl, mix together the flour and sugar until well combined.

4. In a small bowl, whisk together the heavy cream and vanilla.

5. Slowly add the cream mixture to the flour mixture, mixing until the dough comes together (it will be a tough dough). Refrigerate the dough for 30 to 35 minutes.

6. Roll the dough into golf ball–size balls.

7. Four or five at a time, carefully add the doughnut holes to the oil. Fry the doughnut holes for 2 to 3 minutes per side, until golden brown in color.

8. Once the doughnut holes are golden brown, remove from the oil and place on the cooling rack lined with paper towels.

9. If not serving immediately, place the doughnut holes in a 250-degree oven to keep warm. If serving immediately, drizzle the doughnut holes with honey and sprinkle with crushed pistachios.

HOT LITTLE TIPS

How to Be a Biscuit in the Kitchen: Cooking Together as a Family

My girls love to be with me in the kitchen most days. I like every day to be an adventure, and when you make your kitchen a fun place, even cooking can be an exciting family experience. This can be as simple as trying new ingredients or foods you've never made before or even pretending your kitchen is a restaurant. When my oldest daughter started working at Callie's Hot Little Biscuit, where the kitchen is super tiny, I noticed that when she was back in our home kitchen, she started using the restaurant lingo: "Behind" to mean someone's behind you; "Hot behind" to mean someone's behind you with something hot, so be careful; and "Knife," as in, look where you walk because someone's holding something sharp. The girls feel so grown-up wearing aprons, using the lingo, and making and plating the food. It creates a fun and energetic atmosphere.

Children understandably can be scared to use knives or cook with hot oil. Of course, small children shouldn't be using these, but for older children, I would rather educate them than shelter them. Our guiding principle for this is: *don't be afraid—just be safe.* I've shown my girls the proper way to chop with a knife to avoid their fingers, and when we're frying, we do it together, with me standing over them and guiding them.

It does take more time to prepare a meal when you're also teaching children all the aspects of cooking. Sometimes you're in a hurry and you want to do it yourself, but I've discovered with my girls that taking that extra bit of time to teach them, and then letting them try, make mistakes, and learn, gives them so much confidence! Now they can plan and make a meal for me and my husband on their own. That's a night off for us, and it gives the girls pride in their work. We sit down at the table, and everyone is happy.

Knife Tips for Kids

- Let them practice without worrying about doing it wrong or wasting ingredients. Start with a slice of vegetable you've already cut that they can cut into smaller pieces, or something soft like a banana.
- Show them how to choke up on the knife, putting their hand where the handle meets the blade, for better control.
- Demonstrate the bear claw grip to protect their fingers. First, form your noncutting hand into a bear claw, with fingers and thumbs curled. Then place your curled fingers on top of the veggie to be sliced, with fingertips on the veggie, knuckles facing out, and thumb on the side and slightly behind to hold the veggie steady.

Frying Tips for Kids

- Never fill a pot more than two-thirds full of cooking oil.
- Always keep a thermometer in the oil and make sure the temperature stays between 350 and 370 degrees.
- Instead of dropping food into the hot oil, which can splash, lower food into the oil using a wire skimmer/strainer or tongs.
- Avoid putting too much food in the oil at a time.

UNEXPECTED CREATIONS FROM LEFTOVER BISCUITS AND DOUGH

SAVORY SOUTHERN BISCUIT CASSEROLE

We came up with the idea for biscuit casseroles at Callie's Hot Little Biscuit as a way to use leftover biscuits on the days we didn't sell out. At first, we only sold the casseroles during the holidays, but the demand was so high we now sell them year-round. You may even want to whip up some extra biscuits on purpose to make the casseroles.

Makes 6 to 8 servings

3 cups cubed leftover buttermilk biscuits, cut into $1/2$-inch to 1-inch cubes (about 4 to 5 biscuits)

1 cup cooked ground sausage

$1/4$ cup finely chopped green onions (2 to 3 green onions)

1 cup shredded Cheddar cheese (4-ounce block)

1 $1/2$ cups whole milk

3 large eggs

$1/2$ teaspoon dry mustard

1 teaspoon salt

$1/2$ teaspoon freshly ground coarse black pepper

1. Preheat the oven to 300 degrees. Toast the cubed biscuits in the oven for 15 minutes, then let them cool.

2. Increase the oven temperature to 350 degrees.

3. Grease a 9-inch cast-iron skillet or 8 x 8-inch casserole dish.

4. In a large bowl, toss together the toasted biscuit cubes, ground sausage, green onions, and Cheddar cheese. Transfer the mixture to the skillet or dish.

5. In a small bowl, whisk together the milk, eggs, dry mustard, salt, and pepper. Pour the mixture over the biscuits in the skillet or dish, making sure all the pieces are coated.

6. Cover the skillet or dish with foil and let it sit for 30 minutes.

7. Bake, covered in foil, for 20 minutes, until the liquid is set. Remove the foil and bake 10 to 20 minutes longer, until the casserole is golden brown on top.

HOT LITTLE TIP

Freshly Grate Your Cheese

Pre-shredded cheese contains anticlumping additives and preservatives that prevent the cheese from melting as it should. I buy my Cheddar and Monterey Jack in blocks, shred it in the food processor, and then keep it in plastic bags for a few days until I'm ready to use it. It's just better—and cheaper. One 8-ounce block yields 2 cups of shredded cheese.

TOASTED MAPLE BISCUIT CASSEROLE

Here's the sweet version, using leftover cinnamon biscuits.

Makes 6 to 8 servings

4 cups cubed leftover cinnamon biscuits, cut into ½-inch to 1-inch cubes (about 5 to 6 biscuits)

1 ½ cups whole milk

3 large eggs

¼ cup maple syrup

1 ½ teaspoons ground cinnamon

½ teaspoon vanilla extract

½ teaspoon salt

1 tablespoon cinnamon topping (see below)

1 teaspoon turbinado sugar

CINNAMON TOPPING

¾ cup white sugar

¾ cup firmly packed light brown sugar

6 tablespoons ground cinnamon

1. Preheat the oven to 300 degrees. Toast the cubed biscuits in the oven for 15 minutes, then let them cool.

2. In the meantime, make the cinnamon topping by combining the white sugar, brown sugar, and cinnamon in a small bowl. You will not need all of the topping for this recipe. You can save what's left and use it to top anything from toast to biscuit doughnut holes.

3. Increase the oven temperature to 350 degrees.

4. Grease a 9-inch cast-iron skillet or 8 x 8-inch casserole dish.

5. Line the bottom of the skillet or dish with the toasted biscuit cubes.

6. In a small bowl, whisk together the milk, eggs, maple syrup, cinnamon, vanilla, and salt. Pour the mixture over the biscuits in the skillet or dish, making sure all the pieces are coated.

7. Top with the cinnamon topping and turbinado sugar. Cover the skillet or dish with foil and let it sit for 30 minutes.

8. Bake, covered in foil, for 20 minutes, until the liquid is set. Remove the foil and bake 10 to 20 minutes longer, until the casserole is golden brown on top.

BISCUIT BOWLS

I was at a food show before opening Callie's Hot Little Biscuit, and I noticed people eating edible bowls. Bread bowls were nothing new for serving soup, but these bread bowls held grits. That sparked an idea: we could make *biscuit* bowls to serve the grits at Callie's Hot Little Biscuit. I'd wanted to have grits on the menu, but I didn't want to use paper bowls. Now I had my solution. But when we tried to make bowls from the biscuit dough, they were too delicate and fell apart. That led us to an even better idea: use the leftover biscuit dough. After two roll-outs, the leftover dough was tougher and sturdier. You can use these bowls for grits, soup, ice cream sundaes, or as a base for a sweet pie, macaroni pie, or tomato pie. Fill them, then eat them!

Note: The number of bowls this recipe makes depends on how much leftover dough you're using.

I like to use an empty quart storage container to cut out the dough. You can use a similar container or the rim of a jar, or you can even form the dough into circles by hand.

Leftover buttermilk biscuit dough	Nonstick cooking spray	Flour for work surface

1. Preheat the oven to 350 degrees. Spray nonstick cooking spray on *the back side* of a muffin pan.
2. Flour your work surface generously. Roll out the dough to $1/4$-inch thickness.
3. Using the top of an open quart container, stamp out circles from the dough. Place the circles on the back side of the muffin pan over the muffin cups, using the cups to mold the dough.
4. Bake for 8 to 10 minutes, or until the bowls are very light in color.
5. Allow the bowls to cool at room temperature and either use them or wrap them in aluminum foil and freeze for future use.

HOT LITTLE TIP

These freeze beautifully. Simply wrap in foil and reheat before filling!

BISCUIT CRACKERS

I've always loved artisan crackers, and at Callie's Hot Little Biscuit I didn't want to serve our pimento cheese with potato chips or something we didn't make ourselves. Enter the biscuit cracker, another fantastic way to repurpose leftover dough. These are delicious and super crunchy, and they last forever. You can even make a sweet cracker by substituting cinnamon sugar for the salt and pepper. Use these for pimento cheese, in a crudités, or simply when you want a bite with a little crunch.

Note: The number of crackers this recipe makes depends on how much leftover dough you're using.

Third roll-out of buttermilk biscuit dough or other leftover buttermilk

biscuit dough
Melted butter (amount will depend on how much dough you're using)

Salt
Freshly ground coarse black pepper

1. Preheat the oven to 350 degrees.
2. Roll out the dough to about ⅛-inch thickness (as thin as you can get it).
3. Slice the dough into rustic strips and transfer them to a rimmed baking sheet lined with parchment paper.
4. Poke holes in the strips with a fork.
5. Brush melted butter onto the strips and sprinkle with salt and pepper.
6. Bake for 10 to 15 minutes, or until browned and crisp. Thinner strips crisp quickly; thicker strips will take more time.
7. Let the crackers cool, then store in a sealed container.

EGGS IN A HOLE

My dear friend Brian Hart Hoffman, president of Hoffman Media, asked me to fly to Los Angeles with him to go to brunch at Ellen Bennett's. Ellen is the founder of Hedley & Bennett, a company that makes handmade aprons in LA. She hosts brunches for fifteen to twenty people who don't know each other. All of us walked into Ellen's house at 10:00 a.m. on a Sunday and just started cooking. Then we sat on blankets in the backyard and ate. The experience was yet another amazing example of how food brings people together. As we broke bread together in a stranger's home, everyone contributing something to eat, any barriers between us came down and we could enjoy each other's company. I taught everyone how to make biscuits and then used the leftover dough to make Eggs in a Hole. I was only in LA for a total of thirty-six hours, but I left feeling uplifted, savoring the feeling of sharing friendship and goodwill through food, sunshine, and hands working together in the kitchen.

Note: The number of servings this recipe makes depends on how much leftover dough you're using. Also, for this particular recipe, I like to use medium-size eggs rather than large, if I have them.

Leftover buttermilk biscuit dough from stamping out biscuits

Melted butter (amount will depend on how much dough you're using)

Eggs (one per biscuit cutout)

Freshly ground coarse black pepper

Salt

1. After making biscuits, reduce the oven temperature to 400 degrees and line a rimmed baking sheet with parchment paper.

2. Transfer the leftover biscuit dough to the baking sheet after all twelve biscuits have been stamped out. You now have your "nest."

3. Brush the nest with melted butter and bake for 12 minutes.

4. Pull the biscuit nest out of the oven and crack an egg inside each biscuit cutout.

5. Bake for an additional 7 minutes, or until the egg reaches your preference of doneness.

6. Brush with melted butter again, then sprinkle with salt and pepper and serve.

HOT LITTLE TIP

As a great way to add flavor and color, I top this dish with shredded cheese and any fresh herbs I have on hand.

SPRING

Spring is when everyone comes out of their shell. After hibernating inside and the indulgence of comfort food, I am ready for a rebirth. Ready to try new things, to go outside and explore everything that is fresh in the world.

As the bright spring colors come back into the produce, my imagination races with all the possibilities. Venturing out on spring break excursions is another huge inspiration for me. Traveling and getting to know different cultures is where I get most of my food ideas. I also love to take my own food traditions with me when I travel. In my family, what we eat is always what we remember most, whether we're talking about holiday traditions, like having lamb on Easter, or the trips we have taken and what we ate while we were away from home. So when I travel, I like to take food with me to prepare at least one or two meals, and when I return home, I like to re-create the amazing new food adventures we experienced. It becomes this lovely melding of old traditions and new ingredients and methods, flavored with the beautiful zest of the people and places we visited.

For me, spring is that exciting transition from old to new and all the possibilities in between—trying new combinations of flavors, unusual vegetables at the farmers market, and fresh herbs missed during the winter. It all comes together in recipes full of color and flavor that awaken us from our winter's sleep and activate our taste buds and imagination.

WEEKNIGHT SUPPERS

Spatchcock Chicken with Peruvian-Style Green Sauce

Tomato Rice Bake with Smoked Sausage

Cacio e Pepe

Artichoke Soup

Citrus Soy Chicken Skewers with Peanut Sauce

Mediterranean Shrimp Orzo (or Dip!)

WEEKEND SUPPERS

Pork al Pastor

Jerk Chicken

Salmon Salad with the Nuns

Crab Cakes

Snapper with Cilantro Chimichurri

Roasted Leg of Lamb

HOT LITTLE EXTRAS

French Feta Dip

Fried Green Tomatoes

Currant Almond Rice

Grilled Asparagus and Green Onions with Yogurt Shallot Sauce

Grapefruit and Avocado Salad

Zucchini Salad

DRINKS AND DESSERTS

Classic Daiquiris

Spiked Arnold Palmers

Cream Cheese Pie

Best Ever Chocolate Pie

WEEKNIGHT
SUPPERS

SPATCHCOCK CHICKEN WITH PERUVIAN-STYLE GREEN SAUCE

My mother used to buy a cut from the butcher called *airline chicken*, which she flattened and cooked with a brick on top. This recipe takes that idea of flattening and applies it to a whole chicken so that it cooks faster. The result is all the moist deliciousness of a Sunday slowly roasted chicken on a weeknight. It's cooked at high heat on a sheet pan, so everything gets crispy, which is a texture I love. You can substitute the veggies for any you have on hand—zucchini, squash, broccoli, okra. You can even substitute the sauce and instead of Peruvian flavors use Greek or Indian spices, with the same cooking method. I will say, though, this particular sauce is highly addictive, visually fabulous, and literally finger-licking good. Another thing about this dish—it's just fun to say "spatchcock."

Makes 4 servings 🕐

2 lemons, 1 sliced and 1 cut in half

1 lime, sliced

3 1/2- to 4-pound whole organic chicken, spatchcocked

(backbone removed by you or your butcher)

2 cups bite-size yellow potato pieces

1 small onion, sliced (about 1/2 cup)

4 cloves garlic, smashed

3 tablespoons olive oil, divided

Salt and freshly ground coarse black pepper to taste

PERUVIAN-STYLE GREEN SAUCE

1 jalapeño pepper, chopped

1 1/2 cups fresh cilantro

2 green onions (white and green parts)

3 cloves garlic

Juice of 1 lime (1 1/2 to 2 tablespoons)

1 tablespoon white vinegar

1/4 cup sour cream

1/2 cup mayonnaise

1 teaspoon cumin

2 tablespoons olive oil

Salt and freshly ground coarse black pepper to taste

1. To make the green sauce: In a food processor, combine the jalapeño, cilantro, green onions, garlic, lime juice, vinegar, sour cream, mayonnaise, cumin, olive oil, and salt and pepper. Pulse until the mixture is combined and smooth. Refrigerate until ready to use. It will thicken a bit while chilling.

2. Preheat the oven to 450 degrees. Put foil on one half of a large rimmed baking sheet. Fold the edge of the foil up to create a border over half of the baking sheet.

3. Place the sliced lemon and lime in the middle of the foil side of the baking sheet.

4. If you are removing the backbone of the chicken yourself, place the whole chicken, breast side down, on a cutting board. Start at the thigh end and cut

along the backbone on one side. Turn the chicken around and cut from the wing to drumstick side along the other side of the backbone. Remove the backbone and save it to make stock. Flip the chicken back over, breast side up. Push on the breastbone to flatten the chicken. You will hear a cracking sound. Place it on top of the lemon and lime slices, breast side up, and gently separate the skin from the meat as best you can.

5. Squeeze the juice from the lemon halves all over the chicken. In a medium bowl, toss the potatoes with the onions, garlic, and 2 tablespoons of the olive oil. Arrange the potatoes, onions, and garlic on the half of the pan without the foil. You will have the chicken on the foil side of the pan and the potatoes, onions, and garlic on the other side of the pan. The foil border will keep the chicken

juices from soaking into the potatoes as they cook. Drizzle the remaining tablespoon of olive oil on the chicken. Season everything with a generous amount of salt and pepper.

6. Bake for 50 to 60 minutes, or until the internal temperature of the chicken reaches 165 degrees. Every 20 minutes, turn the potatoes to crisp on all sides. Watch the potatoes and onions along the edges of the pan as the sides heat up more than the pan's center. For extra-crispy chicken skin, after baking, remove the potatoes and onions from the pan, then broil the chicken on high heat for 3 to 5 minutes.

7. Remove the chicken from the oven and let it rest for 10 minutes before carving.

8. Serve with the Peruvian-Style Green Sauce on the side.

Note: For the yellow potatoes, you will need about 1 pound. I recommend using Yukon Gold, Yellow Finn, or German Butterball.

TOMATO RICE BAKE WITH SMOKED SAUSAGE

Red rice is a traditional Southern dish (and a tradition in other cultures as well), and I love the nostalgia of it. This version is an update that makes it into an easy one-pot meal where you don't have to cook the rice ahead of time. And there are so many variations. You can add cheese. You can serve it as a side instead of a main. You can make a vegetarian version. My children love it. My favorite thing is the way the rice gets crispy on top. It gives the dish that extra bite and texture that makes me happy.

Makes 8 to 10 servings

6 slices bacon

1 yellow onion, diced
(about 1 cup)

3 celery stalks, diced
(about 1 ½ cups)

1 green bell pepper,
diced (about 1 cup)

4 cloves garlic, minced
(about 4 teaspoons)

1 (28-ounce) can
crushed tomatoes

1 tablespoon dried oregano

1 teaspoon crushed red
pepper flakes

1 ½ cups basmati rice,
rinsed 4 to 5 times in
cold water and drained

1 cup water or chicken
stock (can substitute
vegetable stock)

1 teaspoon lemon juice

Salt and freshly ground
coarse black
pepper to taste

3 tablespoons butter,
divided

1 (14-ounce) package

smoked sausage, cut
into ½-inch pieces

1 cup fresh bread crumbs

> ## HOT LITTLE TIP
>
> ### Make It Veg Friendly
>
> For a vegetarian version of this dish, skip the bacon and sausage and substitute 2 tablespoons of olive oil for the bacon grease.

1. Preheat the oven to 350 degrees.

2. Heat a cast-iron skillet or other oven-safe skillet to medium heat. Add the bacon and cook until crisp. Remove the bacon from the skillet and drain on paper towels. Remove all but 2 tablespoons of the bacon grease from the skillet. When the bacon is cool, crumble it and set aside.

3. In the same skillet with 2 tablespoons of bacon grease, add the onions, celery, bell peppers, and garlic. Sauté for 5 to 7 minutes, or until the vegetables are tender. Remove from the heat.

4. Transfer the vegetables to a large bowl. Add the tomatoes, oregano, red

pepper flakes, rice, water, lemon juice, crumbled bacon, and salt and pepper. Stir to combine.

5. Add 1 tablespoon of the butter to the same cast-iron skillet over medium heat. Once the butter has melted, pour in the rice mixture. Add the smoked sausage slices and top with bread crumbs. Dot the remaining 2 tablespoons of butter all over the bread crumbs.

6. Cover with foil and bake for 45 to 60 minutes. Remove the foil and broil for 4 to 6 minutes to toast the bread crumbs and crisp the sausage.

CACIO E PEPE

My oldest daughter, Caroline, likes to invite her friends over for Saturday night dinner parties. Considering what she could be getting up to as a sixteen-year-old, I'm all for it! I buy the ingredients, and she and her friends cook the meal and clean up afterward. She started out by making carbonara, but folding an egg into hot pasta is challenging for any cook and can lead to scrambled egg pasta! So I suggested Cacio e Pepe, which, in my opinion, is not only easier but also tastier! It's decadent and delicious.

Makes 4 to 6 servings

4 tablespoons butter

1 tablespoon freshly ground coarse black pepper

4 ounces pancetta, diced

1 cup finely diced sweet onion

1 (12-ounce) package bucatini pasta

2 cups grated Parmesan cheese

1 cup grated Romano cheese

1 to 1 1/2 cups reserved pasta water

1. In a small skillet over medium heat, melt the butter and sauté the pepper until toasted and fragrant.

2. In a large skillet over medium heat, sauté the pancetta until it renders fat and begins to crisp.

3. Add the onions to the skillet and cook until they are golden in color and softened.

4. Boil the pasta in salted water and cook according to the directions on the box for al dente. Before you drain the pasta, reserve 2 cups of the pasta water and set aside. Drain the pasta and return it to the pot.

5. Add the Parmesan and Romano cheeses to the pasta and mix to combine.

6. Add the pasta water slowly to form the sauce.

7. Add the pancetta and onions and mix well.

8. Add the black pepper and butter and mix well.

9. Taste for seasonings. Add more pasta water if needed.

10. Serve in warm bowls.

HOT LITTLE TIP

This makes for an elevated, decadent weekend meal too! Perfect for date night.

ARTICHOKE SOUP

This soup is velvety and rich. It's one of those soups that tastes even better the second day, so I usually make it a day ahead. It's elegant enough for a dinner party but simple enough for a weeknight meal. I like to serve it with a crusty crouton on top and a green salad on the side. Think it's impossible to get your children to voluntarily eat artichokes? This creamy, delicious soup is a great way to get them started. My girls love it!

Makes 8 to 10 servings (11 cups total)

3 (14-ounce) cans
quartered artichoke
hearts, drained
and rinsed
4 cloves garlic, smashed
2 tablespoons olive oil
Salt and freshly ground
coarse black
pepper to taste
4 slices uncooked bacon,
cut into bite-size pieces
2 medium shallots, diced
(about 6 tablespoons)

8 cups chicken stock
2 ½ cups heavy
whipping cream
Bundle of fresh thyme, tied
with kitchen twine and
reserving 1 tablespoon
thyme leaves for
garnish (12 stems)
Parmesan cheese rind (3-
to 4-inch section, or
more if preferred)
Zest of 1 lemon (about
2 teaspoons)

> ## HOT LITTLE TIP
>
> ### Make It Veg Friendly
>
> For a vegetarian version of this dish, skip the bacon and substitute 2 tablespoons of olive oil for the bacon grease.

1. Preheat the oven to 400 degrees. Line a rimmed baking sheet with foil.
2. Place the artichokes and smashed garlic cloves on the foil-lined baking sheet. Drizzle the olive oil over the top and sprinkle with salt and pepper.
3. Bake for 30 minutes, or until the artichokes turn slightly golden brown.
4. Meanwhile, heat a Dutch oven or large pot to medium heat. Add the bacon pieces and cook until the bacon is crisp.
5. Remove the bacon from the Dutch oven and let it drain on paper towels, leaving the bacon grease in the pot.
6. Add the shallots to the bacon grease.

Sauté for 2 to 3 minutes or until the shallots soften.

7. Set aside ¼ cup of the roasted artichokes and the foil-lined baking sheet. Add the remaining roasted artichokes and garlic to the pot. Add the chicken stock, heavy cream, thyme bundle, and Parmesan rind.
8. Simmer for 30 minutes.
9. Remove the Parmesan rind and thyme bundle from the soup. Using an immersion blender, blend the soup until it's smooth. (Or place the soup in a blender, blend until smooth, and return the soup to the pot—but be careful because the

soup will be very hot.) After blending, pour the soup carefully through a sieve to remove the artichoke fibers. Return to the Dutch oven.

10. Add the lemon zest and salt and pepper to taste.

11. Preheat the oven to broil. Place the reserved roasted artichokes on the foil-lined baking sheet in the oven and broil them until just crisp.

12. Serve the soup in bowls garnished with a crouton, the bacon, fresh thyme leaves, and broiled artichoke hearts.

HOT LITTLE TIP

Homemade Croutons

To make croutons, you can use any leftover biscuits or bread. Halve the biscuits or tear the bread into pieces and place in a bowl. Drizzle them with olive oil and sprinkle with salt and pepper and whatever else you have on hand—minced garlic, garlic powder, onion powder. Toss it all together, so the pieces of bread are coated. Dump the pieces onto a rimmed baking sheet and bake at 400 degrees for 15 minutes.

CITRUS SOY CHICKEN SKEWERS WITH PEANUT SAUCE

To save time on weeknights, this peanut sauce skips the traditional steps of roasting and crushing the peanuts and uses peanut butter instead. You don't really need a side for this dish because with all the accoutrements for toppings, it makes a full plate. Still, I never make enough of it—my children always want more. This is a great way to use one of my favorite go-to meats: boneless, skinless chicken thighs. They cook quickly and have a little fat on them, so they get a great charred texture from the grill.

Makes 6 skewers

1 tablespoon minced garlic (about 6 cloves)

1 tablespoon minced fresh ginger (a 1- to 2-inch piece of ginger, peeled)

1 tablespoon minced lemongrass (a 4-inch piece of lemongrass about 1/4 inch wide)

1 tablespoon fish sauce

1 tablespoon soy sauce

Zest and juice of 1 lime (about 1 teaspoon zest and 1 1/2 to 2 tablespoons juice)

1 1/2 pounds boneless, skinless chicken thighs (about 5 thighs)

Metal or wooden skewers

Vegetable or canola oil

Butter lettuce or cooked rice to serve

HOT LITTLE TIP

Zest the citrus before cutting and juicing it.

Peanut Sauce

1/2 cup peanut butter

5 (1-inch) chunks of fresh pineapple

2 tablespoons soy sauce

2 tablespoons water

1 tablespoon fish sauce

1 tablespoon hoisin sauce

1 shallot, chopped (1 to 2 tablespoons)

1 tablespoon minced fresh ginger (a 1- to 2-inch piece of ginger, peeled)

1 teaspoon chili garlic paste

Zest and juice of 1 lime (about 1 teaspoon zest and 1 1/2 to 2 tablespoons juice)

Garnish

Chopped peanuts

Chopped green onions

Chopped fresh cilantro

Chopped fresh basil

Chopped fresh mint

Minced red onion

1. In a large resealable plastic bag, combine the garlic, ginger, lemongrass, fish sauce, soy sauce, lime zest, and lime juice. Cut the chicken thighs into strips and add them to the bag. Massage the chicken to make sure it is well coated. Place the bag in the refrigerator and marinate the chicken for 30 to 60

minutes, turning the chicken every 15 minutes. If you are using wooden skewers, put them in water to soak for 30 minutes.

2. While the chicken marinates, make the peanut sauce. In a food processor, combine the peanut butter, pineapple, soy sauce, water, fish sauce, hoisin sauce, shallot, ginger, chili garlic paste, lime zest, and lime juice. Pulse until combined and smooth.

3. Once the chicken finishes marinating,

preheat the grill to 450 degrees. Then thread the chicken onto the skewers. Rub the grill grates with vegetable or canola oil.

4. Grill the chicken skewers until the internal temperature reaches 165 degrees, about 4 to 5 minutes per side.

5. Serve the skewers over lettuce or rice and top with the chopped peanuts, green onions, cilantro, basil, mint, red onions, and peanut sauce.

HOT LITTLE TIP

Serve Plenty of Toppings

Toppings and what I call "accoutrements" make food more fun and flavorful. When I look at a dish, I ask myself, *Does it have texture, color, a fresh appeal? Does it need salt, acid, or heat?* Fresh-minced herbs, chopped nuts, toasted bread crumbs, green onions, fresh lime juice, and jalapeño slices are just some ideas for toppings that each person can sprinkle on their plate and customize to their taste. And kids love toppings!

MEDITERRANEAN SHRIMP ORZO (OR DIP!)

My mother has been making this Mediterranean shrimp for thirty years, so its flavor represents a sweet memory for me. When she made it for supper at home, she would toss it with orzo, but the dip version has been a staple of her catering business for years. I was reminded of this dish during the COVID-19 quarantine, when she brought the dip over as an appetizer for a socially distanced supper. If quarantine has any silver linings, one of them is the food memories from all the cooking we did!

Makes 6 to 8 servings   (W)

- 2 tablespoons olive oil
- 4 large tomatoes, diced (about 4 to 5 cups)
- 3/4 cup chopped Kalamata olives
- 1/2 red onion, diced (about 1/2 cup)
- 2 cloves garlic, minced (about 2 teaspoons)
- 2 tablespoons chopped fresh dill
- Zest and juice of 1/2 lemon (about 1 teaspoon zest and 1 to 1 1/2 tablespoons juice)
- 1 pound fresh shrimp, peeled, deveined, and chopped into thirds
- 2 cups cooked orzo
- 1/2 cup crumbled feta cheese
- 2 tablespoons chopped fresh flat-leaf Italian parsley (about 6 stems)
- Salt and freshly ground coarse black pepper to taste
- Naan (page 171) and/or pita bread for serving

1. In a cast-iron skillet or sauté pan, heat the olive oil over medium heat.
2. Add the tomatoes, olives, red onions, garlic, dill, lemon zest, and lemon juice. Sauté for 5 minutes. Add the shrimp and sauté until shrimp are cooked through, about 3 to 4 minutes. They should be pink and opaque.
3. Remove from the heat. Pour the shrimp mixture into a large bowl. Add the orzo, feta cheese, parsley, and salt and pepper. Toss to coat and serve at room temperature with naan and/or pita bread.

As a Dip

- 4 large tomatoes, diced (about 4 to 5 cups)
- 3/4 cup chopped Kalamata olives
- 1/2 red onion, diced (about 1/2 cup)
- 2 cloves garlic, minced (about 2 teaspoons)
- 2 tablespoons chopped fresh dill
- Zest and juice of 1/2 lemon (about 1 teaspoon zest and 1 to 1 1/2 tablespoons juice)
- 1/2 cup feta cheese
- Salt and freshly ground coarse black pepper to taste
- 1 pound fresh shrimp, peeled, deveined, and chopped into thirds
- 2 tablespoons chopped fresh flat-leaf Italian parsley (about 6 stems)
- Naan (page 171) and/or pita bread for serving

1. Preheat the oven to 425 degrees.

2. In a large bowl, combine the tomatoes, olives, red onions, garlic, dill, lemon zest, lemon juice, feta cheese, and salt and pepper.

3. Pour the mixture into a cast-iron skillet. Bake for 6 to 8 minutes to soften the tomatoes and onions and blend the flavors. Stir in the chopped shrimp and cook 2 to 3 minutes until the shrimp are pink and opaque.

4. Turn the oven broiler to high heat. Broil for 2 minutes, or until the feta is brown and bubbly.

5. Remove the skillet from the oven and garnish with fresh parsley. Serve with toasted naan and/or pita bread.

WEEKEND
SUPPERS

PORK AL PASTOR

When we were on a family vacation in Mexico for spring break, we stopped to eat at a roadside restaurant and had one of the best meals we'd ever had. It was Pork al Pastor, with the cooks carving the meat right off the spits. I couldn't wait to try to re-create it at home. Pineapple is usually too sweet for me, but in this dish it's the perfect complement to the pork, with the sugar running down the meat and charring the edges as it cooks. The home method does take a little patience, with wooden skewers in place of the spit, but the flavor is well worth the effort.

Makes 4 to 6 servings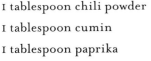

I tablespoon chili powder

I tablespoon cumin

I tablespoon paprika

I tablespoon dried oregano

I teaspoon cayenne pepper

I tablespoon salt

Freshly ground coarse
   black pepper to taste

I (3-pound) boneless
   pork butt

6 cloves garlic, minced
   (about 6 teaspoons)

1/2 cup cider vinegar

I cup freshly squeezed
   orange juice (about
   4 to 5 oranges)

I whole pineapple

4 wooden skewers

Chopped cilantro
   for garnish

Chopped white onion
   for garnish

Fresh salsa to serve

1. In a small bowl, combine the chili powder, cumin, paprika, oregano, cayenne pepper, salt, and pepper.

2. Cut the pork butt into 1/2-inch thick slices and then cut those slices in half.

3. Place the sliced pork into a gallon-size resealable plastic bag. Add the chili powder mixture to the pork and use your hands to coat all of the pieces on both sides as evenly as possible.

4. Add the garlic, vinegar, and orange juice to the bag. Seal the bag and gently shake it to make sure everything is mixed together.

5. Marinate the pork in the refrigerator for 24 hours.

6. Remove all of the oven racks except for one, placed at the lowest setting. Preheat the oven to 375 degrees.

7. Cut the pineapple, leaving about 3 inches on the bottom as a base, and remove the top. Cut the middle part into 2-inch thick pieces. Reserve the pineapple top and half of the 2-inch middle pieces for serving.

8. On a cutting board or work surface, place the bottom of the pineapple flat side down. Place the 4 skewers in a square shape into the pineapple.

9. Alternate threading slices of meat and pineapple pieces onto each skewer, pushing down the meat into the pineapple and being sure to evenly divide the meat and pineapple among the four skewers.

10. Place the pineapple in a deep roasting pan. Arrange foil "balls" around the pineapple so it does not tip over. Bake

for 1 hour, then place foil on top of the meat so it does not burn. Bake an additional 1 to 1 ½ hours, or until an inserted meat thermometer reads 165 degrees.

11. Let the meat cool slightly, then place it on a platter. Add the pineapple top back on top of the pork. Shave the meat off of the pineapple with a knife. For any pieces that did not get crisp, especially pieces cut from the inside, place those slices on a foil-lined rimmed baking sheet and broil so they get crispy.

12. Serve with the reserved pineapple chunks, cilantro, onions, and fresh salsa.

JERK CHICKEN

When I'm craving a tropical vacation, this Jerk Chicken transports my imagination and taste buds to the Caribbean, at least temporarily! The only hard part about this recipe is putting together the enormous amount of herbs and spices. I like to mix them up ahead of time when I can. I love to serve this dish with Currant Almond Rice (page 73) for an easy Sunday supper.

Makes 4 to 6 servings (W)

5 bay leaves, crumbled then chopped

1 teaspoon cayenne pepper

1 teaspoon ground cinnamon

1 teaspoon ground nutmeg

1 teaspoon salt

2 teaspoons ground ginger

1 tablespoon allspice

1 tablespoon garlic powder

1 tablespoon onion powder

1 tablespoon chopped fresh rosemary

1 tablespoon chopped fresh thyme

2 tablespoons firmly packed light brown sugar

2 tablespoons turbinado sugar

2 tablespoons white vinegar

Zest and juice of 2 limes

(about 2 teaspoons zest and 3 to 4 tablespoons juice)

½ cup olive oil

Salt and freshly ground coarse black pepper to taste

1 whole chicken, cut into 8 pieces (or 8 chicken pieces of your preference)

....

1. In a small bowl, combine the bay leaves, cayenne pepper, cinnamon, nutmeg, salt, ginger, allspice, garlic powder, onion powder, rosemary, thyme, brown sugar, and turbinado sugar.

2. In a large bowl, whisk together the vinegar, lime zest, lime juice, and olive oil. Add the spice mixture and mix until well combined and a paste forms.

3. Liberally salt and pepper the chicken pieces on both sides. Rub the spice mixture all over each piece of chicken. Refrigerate overnight.

4. Bring the chicken to room temperature and grill until the internal temperature reaches 165 degrees. Or you can bake the chicken in the oven at 350 degrees for 60 to 75 minutes, or until the internal temperature is 165 degrees.

SALMON SALAD WITH THE NUNS

Here's another story from our Mexico trip. I usually don't blow-dry my hair because it takes too long, so when I'm on vacation, one of my guilty pleasures is to blow-dry my hair while I sit on the bed and watch TV. I had the TV muted, but I could see that it was a cooking show where nuns were making a raw salmon salad with boiled potatoes and avocado. Nuns. On a cooking show. Making salmon salad with potatoes and avocado. It was unexpected in every way. I just had to make it for myself back home. I sear the salmon instead of serving it raw, and I lightly fry the potato rounds for texture. It makes a beautiful dish inspired by the cooking nuns. I never would have considered putting these flavors together, but the result is heavenly.

Makes 6 to 8 servings

4 medium potatoes,
    peeled and sliced
    ¹/₂ inch thick
¹/₂ cup plus 2 tablespoons
    olive oil plus more for
    drizzling, divided

Salt and freshly ground
    coarse black
    pepper to taste
2 pounds salmon,
    patted dry
Juice of ¹/₂ lime

2 avocados, sliced
1 head butter or Bibb
    lettuce, chopped
¹/₃ cup pepitas (pumpkin
    seeds), roasted
    and salted

CREMA SAUCE

2 cups Mexican crema
    (can substitute yogurt
    or crème fraîche)
4 ramps, washed and

    soaked, trimmed,
    and finely chopped
¹/₄ cup chopped shallots
¹/₃ cup chopped fresh dill

Zest of 1 lime (about
    1 teaspoon)
¹/₂ teaspoon salt
¹/₄ teaspoon freshly ground
    coarse black pepper

1. To make the crema sauce: In a small mixing bowl, combine the crema, ramps, shallots, dill, lime zest, salt, and pepper. Refrigerate for at least 30 minutes, to allow the flavors to meld.

2. In a medium pot, combine the potatoes and just enough water to cover them. Boil the potatoes over high heat until fork tender, being careful not to overcook them. Drain the potatoes and set aside.

3. In a cast-iron skillet or sauté pan, heat ¹/₂ cup of the olive oil over medium-high heat. Add the potatoes and cook for 3 to 4 minutes on both sides until golden brown and crisp. Remove the potatoes from the pan and place them on a paper towel–lined plate. Wipe out the skillet.

4. Heat 2 tablespoons of the olive oil in the same skillet over medium-high heat. Liberally salt and pepper the salmon. Place the salmon skin side up in the

skillet and sear for 2 to 3 minutes on each side, or until the desired temperature is reached. (I like mine medium rare.) Remove the salmon from the skillet. Let it rest for 5 minutes and then cut it into 1-inch pieces.

5. To assemble the salad: Drizzle a little olive oil and sprinkle salt and pepper over the bottom of a serving platter. Layer the potatoes first and drizzle a little more olive oil and salt and pepper. Squeeze the juice from half a lime over the top of the avocado slices. Then layer the avocado slices followed by a drizzle of olive oil and salt and pepper, layer the lettuce with a drizzle of olive oil and salt and pepper, half the crema sauce, the salmon with a drizzle of oil and salt and

pepper, remaining crema sauce, and, finally, roasted pepitas on top.

HOT LITTLE TIPS

Other Uses for Crema
You can also make the crema sauce the day before and refrigerate it overnight. It will continue to grow in flavor! Save it and use it as a mayo on a sandwich, toasted biscuits, or leftover salmon.

Pom for Pop
Garnish this salad with pomegranate seeds for added color, tartness, and zing!

Note: I think it is best to soak the ramps in water for at least 20 minutes before trimming and chopping—they are dirty! Then dry them thoroughly before chopping. If ramps aren't in season, you can use green onions instead.

CRAB CAKES

Crab cakes are one of my and my father's favorite things, and my girls love to crab. We go to my mother's dock and tie chicken necks to long pieces of string. Then we toss them out in the water and wait to feel the tug and bump of a crab on the chicken neck. Slowly, patiently, we pull the line in, little by little, until we can just make out the body of the crab, and someone scoops it up from behind with a net. Luckily, it doesn't take a lot of crab to make crab cakes, so a day of crabbing provides plenty. Feel free to substitute tartar sauce for the remoulade, but don't let the smoking part of the remoulade recipe scare you off. It's super easy and so delicious. You don't have to have a smoker. You can smoke the tomatoes on a charcoal grill—the juices from the tomatoes landing on the coals will create smoke. You can even substitute two tomatoes from a can of fire-roasted tomatoes, but they won't have the same depth of smoky flavor.

Makes 6 crab cakes Ⓦ

- I large egg
- 1/2 cup mayonnaise
- 3 green onions, chopped
- I tablespoon Dijon mustard
- Zest of I lemon (about 2 teaspoons)
- I teaspoon Worcestershire sauce
- I teaspoon minced fresh flat-leaf Italian parsley (about 4 stems)
- I teaspoon hot sauce
- Salt and freshly ground coarse black pepper to taste
- I pound claw crabmeat
- 2 cups bread crumbs, divided
- I tablespoon butter
- 2 tablespoons canola oil

HOT LITTLE TIP

Crabmeat Tips

It takes about eight crabs to come up with a pound of crabmeat. Fall is the best time for crabbing, when there are more and bigger crabs. If you aren't catching your own, you can make this dish more economical by using backfin crabmeat or a combination of backfin and claw meat.

SMOKED TOMATO REMOULADE SAUCE

- 2 tomatoes (if not smoking, you can substitute 2 tomatoes from a can of fire-roasted tomatoes, drained)
- 2 teaspoons dried oregano
- Salt and freshly ground coarse black pepper to taste
- 4 teaspoons olive oil
- 2 cloves garlic, minced
- (about 2 teaspoons or add more to taste)
- 1/2 cup mayonnaise
- 1/2 cup sour cream
- I 1/2 teaspoons capers
- I teaspoon hot sauce

1. To make the sauce: Heat a smoker to 200 degrees. Slice the tomatoes in half. Sprinkle each half with oregano and salt and pepper. Drizzle olive oil on each tomato half. Place the tomato halves face down on the smoker. Smoke for I to 2

hours, or until tender and most of the liquid has drained out. Roughly chop the smoked tomatoes and add them to a large bowl. Add the garlic, mayonnaise, sour cream, capers, and hot sauce. Stir to combine. Serve immediately with the crab cakes or cover with plastic wrap and chill in the refrigerator until ready to use.

2. In a large bowl, whisk together the egg, mayonnaise, green onions, Dijon mustard, lemon zest, Worcestershire, parsley, hot sauce, and salt and pepper. Add the crabmeat and ½ cup of the bread crumbs. Gently stir to combine. Form the mixture into 6 patties.

3. In a small bowl, place the remaining 1 ½ cups of the bread crumbs. Carefully dredge each crab cake into the bread crumbs, coating both sides evenly.

4. Chill the crab cakes in the refrigerator for 30 minutes.

5. In a large skillet, heat the butter and canola oil over medium-high heat. Fry the crab cakes for 3 to 5 minutes per side, or until golden brown and cooked through. Be sure not to overcrowd the pan. You may need to work in two batches.

6. Serve immediately with the Smoked Tomato Remoulade Sauce on the side or drizzled over the crab cakes.

SNAPPER WITH CILANTRO CHIMICHURRI

My daughter Sarah requests this dish all the time. I love snapper for this dish, but you can use other fish. Ask your fishmonger at the fish market what's good and fresh. I ride my bike to Abundant Seafood on Shem Creek and get whatever they recommend. The sauce is luscious and bright—beautiful to taste and to look at on the plate!

HOT LITTLE TIP

Become Best Friends with Your Local Fishmonger and Butcher

The fishmonger at your local seafood market or grocery store knows what is fresh, what looks especially good, what makes a great substitute for other fish, and what methods you can use to cook varieties of seafood you've never tried before. The same thing goes for the butcher. He or she will be delighted to help you. Meat is their specialty, and they're eager to talk to you about it, so tap into their expertise and knowledge of what's good and fresh right now. They can spatchcock your chicken or create other cuts different from what's already in the case. And if something isn't in the case, don't hesitate to ask. They could have a new supply that hasn't been  put out yet. You also can call ahead and ask them to set something aside for you. Make a friend, learn about seafood and meat from the experts, and always be the first one to know when something spectacular comes in.

Makes 4 servings   Ⓦ

1 pound fresh snapper, sliced into 4-ounce portions	Salt and freshly ground coarse black pepper to taste	1 tablespoon olive oil

CILANTRO CHIMICHURRI SAUCE

2 cups loosely packed chopped cilantro (about 2 bunches) 1 cup loosely packed chopped fresh flat-leaf Italian parsley (about 1 bunch) 5 cloves garlic, roughly	chopped (about 5 teaspoons) 3 green onions (both white and green parts), roughly chopped ½ jalapeño pepper, seeds removed and roughly chopped	Juice of ½ lime (about 1 tablespoon) ¼ cup red wine vinegar 1 cup olive oil Salt and freshly ground coarse black pepper to taste

1. To make the cilantro chimichurri sauce: In a food processor, combine the cilantro, parsley, garlic, green onions, and jalapeño. Pulse a few times. Add the lime juice and vinegar and pulse to combine. Slowly add the olive oil while pulsing until the mixture is combined and sauce-like. Season with salt and pepper.

2. Allow the snapper to come to room temperature. Pat the snapper dry with paper towels and season with salt and pepper.

3. In a cast-iron skillet or sauté pan, heat the olive oil over medium-high heat until the surface looks "ripply" but is not smoking. Hold the fillet with tongs and lay the fillet in the skillet away from you. Press down on the fish for 30 to 60 seconds and then let it cook for 3 to 4 minutes on each side, flipping the fish only once without messing with it, or until the fish is cooked through and firm to the touch. Give your pan a shake, and if the fish does not move let it continue to cook.

4. Top the snapper with the chimichurri sauce and serve.

Note: Chimichurri sauce is great with a variety of meats!

ROASTED LEG OF LAMB

This traditional Easter recipe sounds so formal. And it can be if you'd like it to be, but some of my best Easter memories have been eating this lamb off paper plates! This is the ultimate versatile one-pot meal. I've even packed it in a cooler and taken it with us on the boat for Easter Sunday. We anchored at a pretty spot, got out the paper plates, and ate it with our hands. You can take it to the beach. You can have it at a picnic. And by all means, you can serve it with your fine china and crystal! It can be dressed up or down. You can have it however, wherever, whenever it suits you. The slow-roasting cooking method is low maintenance, and the shredded meat easily travels in a container with as much of the gravy as you think is best for serving. It's a surprisingly unfussy meal for all your springtime adventures.

Makes 6 to 8 servings

2 tablespoons bacon
    grease or 1 tablespoon
    butter and 1
    tablespoon olive oil
1 (3- to 4-pound)
    boneless leg of lamb
Salt and freshly ground
    coarse black
    pepper to taste

1/4 cup all-purpose flour
6 carrots, washed,
    peeled, and cut
    into large chunks
1 large yellow onion,
    cut into chunks
12 cloves garlic, peeled
    and smashed
1 cup dry white wine

(sauvignon blanc
    works well)
3 cups chicken stock
7 to 10 sprigs fresh
    rosemary
7 to 10 sprigs fresh flat-
    leaf Italian parsley

1. Preheat the oven to 325 degrees.

2. In a large Dutch oven or pot, heat the bacon grease or butter and oil over high heat.

3. Season the lamb well with salt and pepper. Rub the flour all over the lamb to coat. Add the lamb to the hot pot.

4. Sear the lamb on all sides, about 3 to 4 minutes per side. Once all sides have been seared, remove the lamb and set it aside.

5. In the same pot, combine the carrots, onions, and garlic. Sauté about 4 to 6 minutes to get some color on the onions. Add the wine and bring to a boil. Add the chicken stock. Tie the rosemary and parsley together with kitchen twine and add the herb bundle to the pot. Bring it to a boil. Add the lamb back into the pot.

6. Cover the pot with foil and place a lid on top. Cook in the oven for 2 hours.

7. Remove the lamb from the oven, flip it to the other side, re-cover with foil and the lid, and cook for another hour. Test the lamb by pressing a spoon into the roast—if it feels soft and separates, it is done. If not, continue to cook for 45 minutes.

8. Remove the lamb and carrots from the pot and let the lamb rest for 20 minutes.

9. Place the pot on the stove top and bring the liquid to a boil. Reduce the heat and let it simmer until the liquid thickens into a gravy, about 8 to 12 minutes.

Return the carrots to the pot until warmed. Taste for salt and pepper.

10. Shred the lamb and place it on a serving platter. Spoon the vegetables and gravy on top. Serve immediately and enjoy!

Note: If you are sitting down at a table to eat, I like to serve this with my Pearl Onion and Mushroom Risotto (page 167).

HOT LITTLE TIP

Farmers Market Field Trip

Trips to the farmers market with children can be overwhelming. Sometimes you start with so much excitement, then leave empty-handed and with whiny helpers. I've found that for the most fun and best experience, getting my girls involved in the process and treating the outing like a cultural experience is key. Here are some general tips to keep in mind:

- Send kids on a mission to find something that looks good to them, that they would like to cook at home.
- Give each one their own reusable bag for their selections, so they feel ownership in the process.
- Let them walk around and explore. Encourage them to take a bite when they can and to look at all the colors of the produce and really see for themselves what they would like to try. It's amazing what kids will eat when it's their idea!
- Teach them how to tell if produce is ripe, so when they select something, they pick the best.
- Once they've made their choices, help them follow through at home. Depending on their ages, they may be able to find a recipe and make a dish themselves. Be supportive and open to helping them. You may discover a new family favorite!
- Don't forget the treats. A sno-cone or kettle corn goes a long way in creating a happy field trip.

HOT
LITTLE
EXTRAS

FRENCH FETA DIP

My friend Krysten introduced me to this dip and taught me all about the wonders of French feta. Using the French version in this dip makes all the difference, and you can find it at Whole Foods. Krysten makes this and puts it on a huge board with whole green onions and Persian cucumbers, herbs, and other vegetables. Would you ever want to eat a whole green onion? Covered in this dip, yes!

Makes 4 to 6 servings

$\frac{1}{2}$ cup pine nuts, toasted, divided

2 tablespoons extra-virgin olive oil

7 ounces French feta cheese

$\frac{1}{4}$ cup heavy whipping cream

1 cup sour cream

$\frac{1}{3}$ cup fresh dill

2 cloves garlic

$\frac{1}{2}$ teaspoon lemon zest

1 tablespoon lemon juice

1. In a food processor, combine $\frac{1}{4}$ cup of the pine nuts, olive oil, feta cheese, heavy cream, sour cream, dill, garlic, lemon zest, and lemon juice. Pulse until combined and smooth.

2. Garnish with the remaining $\frac{1}{4}$ cup of the pine nuts and serve.

Note: I like to serve this dip on a crudités platter with carrots, cucumbers, celery, cherry tomatoes, and thinly sliced radishes. It makes a great topping for roasted or baked potatoes and complements most oven-roasted vegetables. Also, I recommend the Valbreso brand for French feta.

FRIED GREEN TOMATOES

Who doesn't love fried green tomatoes? Add some pimento cheese on top, and these make for a perfect stand-alone vegetarian meal.

Makes 6 to 8 servings

2 cups vegetable oil

1 cup all-purpose flour

1 teaspoon salt, plus
    more to taste

1/2 teaspoon freshly ground
    coarse black pepper

1 cup buttermilk

2 large eggs

1/2 cup cornmeal

1/2 cup bread crumbs

1/4 cup finely grated
    Parmesan cheese

1/2 teaspoon cayenne

pepper (or less if
    you don't like heat)

1/2 teaspoon paprika

1/2 teaspoon dry mustard

3 firm green tomatoes,
    cut 1/2 inch thick
    (about 12 slices)

1. Heat the oil in a cast-iron skillet over medium-high heat.

2. While the oil is heating, set up your dipping station with three bowls. In one bowl, season the flour with the salt and pepper. In the second bowl, combine the buttermilk and eggs and whisk to mix. In the third bowl, combine the cornmeal, bread crumbs, Parmesan cheese, cayenne pepper, paprika, and dry mustard.

3. Carefully dip each tomato slice into the flour mixture, then into the egg mixture, and finally into the bread crumb mixture, gently shaking off any excess.

4. Carefully place the tomato slices into the hot oil. Fry only 3 or 4 slices at a time to avoid overcrowding the skillet. Fry for 3 minutes, then flip and fry for 2 minutes, or until golden brown on each side.

5. Remove the tomatoes from the skillet and place on a wire rack or paper towels. Sprinkle each slice with a touch of salt right as it is removed from the oil. Serve immediately.

CURRANT ALMOND RICE

I cook rice to serve with supper a few times a week, so I like to get creative with it every now and then. This rice takes on a whole other identity from plain white rice, with the currants adding a taste that is tart, sweet, and sour all at the same time. If you don't have almonds, substitute walnuts, pistachios, or any nuts you have on hand.

Makes 6 to 8 servings

3 cups chicken broth, vegetable broth, or water

2 cups basmati rice, rinsed 4 to 5 times in cold water and drained

1 cup currants or golden raisins

½ cup slivered almonds, toasted

3 tablespoons salted butter

Salt and freshly ground coarse black pepper to taste

½ cup chopped cilantro

½ cup chopped fresh flat-leaf Italian parsley

1. In a medium saucepan, bring the broth or water to a boil.
2. Add the rice and stir. Cover and reduce the heat to a simmer for 20 minutes, or until the liquid is absorbed and the rice is tender.
3. Once the rice is cooked, scoop it into a large mixing bowl and add the currants or raisins, almonds, and butter. Toss to combine and add salt and pepper to taste. Top with cilantro and parsley to serve.

Note: Use a Charleston rice steamer if you have one.

HOT LITTLE TIP

Charleston Rice Steamer

Rice is my favorite side starch, and the one I make the most. I crave it. I love long-grain, short-grain, basmati, jasmine, and sushi rice. They all have their special place, and they can be dressed up, like my Currant Almond Rice recipe, or served elegantly bare, with only a pat of butter on top. Rice can also bulk up a meal or stretch it out. It's a great staple to have on hand so that your supper can go a little further if you need to add an extra seat at the table.

Rice has been at the heart of Lowcountry cuisine since the late seventeenth century, when the first rice seeds came to the Carolina colony from Madagascar. Rice cultivation flourished under the knowledge, skills, and back-breaking labor of enslaved Africans. It has been a staple of the grandest and the most humble homes in Charleston ever since, and among locals, the Charleston rice steamer is the preferred method for cooking this grain.

Charleston rice steamers are still sold at a few local stores, like Royall Ace Hardware in my neighborhood, as well as online. The steamer is not electric. It works like a double boiler on the stove top. It makes rice that is fluffy and less sticky than rice cooked in a saucepan. There's something comforting about having that steaming pot chugging away on the stove while you prepare the rest of the meal. I highly recommend you give this Charleston contraption a try!

GRILLED ASPARAGUS AND GREEN ONIONS WITH YOGURT SHALLOT SAUCE

It's springtime, and that means I want to grill! I put the asparagus and green onions on the grill while whatever protein I've already grilled is resting. The char is what really makes this dish, plus the sauce. It's hard to believe something so simple packs so much flavor.

Makes 4 to 6 servings

3 tablespoons olive oil

2 bunches asparagus, rinsed and trimmed (about 2 pounds)

2 bunches green onions, rinsed and peeled (6 to 8 green onions)

Salt and freshly ground coarse black pepper to taste

1/2 cup walnuts, roasted in a 350-degree oven for 5 to 7 minutes if whole, less time if chopped

1/3 cup chopped fresh flat-leaf Italian parsley for garnish

YOGURT SHALLOT SAUCE

1 cup plain Greek yogurt

1/2 medium-size shallot, minced (about 1 tablespoon)

1 tablespoon olive oil

Salt and freshly ground coarse black pepper to taste

1. Heat your grill to medium heat.
2. To make the yogurt shallot sauce: In a small bowl, combine the yogurt, shallot, 1 tablespoon olive oil, and salt and pepper to taste. Let it sit on the counter to allow the flavors to meld.
3. Drizzle 3 tablespoons of olive oil over the asparagus and green onions. Sprinkle with salt and pepper.
4. Grill the vegetables for 10 minutes, or until cooked through and slightly charred.
5. Serve the vegetables on a platter and top with the Yogurt Shallot Sauce, roasted walnuts, and fresh parsley.

GRAPEFRUIT AND AVOCADO SALAD

I eat this salad year-round. It's inspired by my mom's recipe, and my girls beg for it at my house and her house. If you don't have the time or ingredients for the vinaigrette, you can instead whisk together ¼ cup of olive oil, the zest and juice of ½ lime, and salt and pepper.

Makes 2 to 4 servings

I head butter lettuce, torn into bite-size pieces (can substitute romaine or Bibb)

I grapefruit, segmented

2 radishes, very thinly sliced into matchsticks

Lime Vinaigrette

I avocado, sliced

¼ cup pepitas (pumpkin

seeds), roasted and salted

Tortilla strips, optional

Cotija cheese, optional

LIME VINAIGRETTE

I tablespoon Dijon mustard

I clove garlic, minced (about I teaspoon)

I teaspoon minced shallot (about I small clove)

Zest and juice of ½ lime (about ½ teaspoon zest and I tablespoon juice)

½ teaspoon chili powder

½ teaspoon cumin

¼ cup olive oil

2 tablespoons white wine vinegar

Salt and freshly ground coarse black pepper to taste

1. To make the lime vinaigrette: In a mason jar or other container, combine the Dijon mustard, garlic, shallot, lime zest, lime juice, chili powder, cumin, olive oil, white wine vinegar, and salt and pepper. Top with a lid and shake until everything is mixed together. Keep refrigerated until ready to use.

2. In a large bowl, combine the lettuce, grapefruit, and radishes. Add the lime vinaigrette (you may not need to use all of the dressing). Toss to coat.

3. To serve, transfer the tossed salad to a serving platter. Top with the avocado slices, roasted pepitas, and, if desired, tortilla strips and Cotija cheese.

Note: For the pepitas, you can substitute sunflower seeds, peanuts, or any seeds or nuts that are salty and crunchy.

HOT LITTLE TIP

How to Segment a Grapefruit

My favorite method is to get John to do it! But if he's not available . . . Place the grapefruit on a cutting board. Remove a slice from the top and the bottom so the grapefruit rests level. Using a sharp paring knife, cut off the peel in sections, following the curve of the grapefruit. If any of the white pith remains, cut that off because it has a bitter taste. Place the knife along the segment line on the side of each section of the grapefruit. Slice through to the center, and the sections will be released. The two keys are a sharp knife and a level fruit!

ZUCCHINI SALAD

Six years ago, my daughter Sarah was diagnosed with epilepsy, so our whole family adopted a keto-type diet. This was before "keto" was a household name or anyone knew what a "zoodle" was. I wanted to figure out how to re-create pasta-like dishes, so I made strips of zucchini using my much-loved Messermeister veggie peeler and created this springtime salad. You can also grate the zucchini on a box grater instead of slicing it into strips, if you'd prefer.

Makes 4 to 6 servings

3 large zucchinis

8 ounces crumbled feta

3 green onions, chopped

1 cup pine nuts, toasted

1/2 cup finely minced red

or green serrano
chili peppers (seeds
and ribs removed)

1/2 cup chopped fresh mint

1/4 cup olive oil

Juice of 1/2 lemon (1 to
1 1/2 tablespoons)

Salt and freshly ground
coarse black
pepper to taste

1. Trim the ends of the zucchini. With a vegetable peeler, shave the zucchini lengthwise into long, wide strips. When you get to the center of the zucchini, turn it over and slice until you get to the center again.

2. In a large bowl, combine the zucchini strips, feta, green onions, pine nuts, serrano chili peppers, mint, olive oil, lemon juice, and salt and pepper. Toss together. Serve immediately for a delicious flavor and crispy texture. Or you can serve it the next day—it will have a softer texture, but the flavor is even better.

DRINKS
AND
DESSERTS

CLASSIC DAIQUIRIS

We love to have food and drink contests with our friend group, and when a "daiq-off" was proposed, to see who could make the best daiquiri, John and I were in. I had already fallen in love with the classic daiquiri served at The Ordinary in Charleston, which is completely different from the frozen concoction with whipped cream and a cherry I'd always thought of. At The Ordinary, they serve the daiquiri in an old-fashioned coupe glass. One time my friends and I even enjoyed enough of them to build a coupe pyramid on our table! For the competition, I pulled out the vintage sorbet glasses passed down to me by John's mother that are kept in their own felt-lined carrying case. We spent an afternoon perfecting the recipe and then packed it in a YETI container, so it would be the perfect temperature for serving. I brought along vintage linen cocktail napkins and the carrying case of special glasses and we poured the daiquiris like pros. We nailed it and won the competition! It really was a win for everyone because these daiquiris are that good.

Makes 1 cocktail

1/2 ounce simple syrup	5 sprigs of mint	2 1/2 ounces good-quality rum
1/4 peach, peeled and sliced	3/4 ounce lime juice	Ice

SIMPLE SYRUP

1 cup sugar	1 cup water

SUGAR SPICE RIM

4 tablespoons sugar	1 1/2 teaspoons cayenne pepper	1 teaspoon smoked paprika
4 teaspoons kosher salt		1 lime wedge

1. To make the simple syrup: In a small saucepan over medium heat, combine the sugar and water. Bring the mixture to a low boil. Stir until the sugar dissolves. Turn off the heat, and let it cool completely. Set aside 1/2 ounce per cocktail, then store the rest in a glass jar in the refrigerator for up to 3 weeks.

2. To make the sugar spice rim: In a small bowl, combine the sugar, salt, cayenne pepper, and paprika. Run the lime wedge over the rim of a coupe or other cocktail glass. Turn the glass upside down and dip the rim into the sugar spice mix. Set aside.

3. In a tall glass, combine the 1/2 ounce of simple syrup, peach, and mint. Muddle together.

4. Add the lime juice and rum. Add ice and cover with a bar shaker. Shake vigorously, then strain into the cocktail glass with the sugar spice rim.

SPIKED ARNOLD PALMERS

John loves to watch the Masters golf tournament, so for a Sunday Funday celebration, we hosted a "Sunday at the Masters" party to get together and watch with friends. We served pimento cheese sandwiches just like they do at the tournament and this frozen alcoholic version of the Arnold Palmer to add some *Cheers!* to the cheering.

Makes 1 cocktail

2 lemon slices, divided
Turbinado sugar
Sweet tea

Lemonade
Rum

Fresh mint plus sprigs
  for garnish
Ice

1. Rub one of the lemon slices around the rim of a tall highball glass.
2. Dip the glass in the turbinado sugar.
3. In a blender, combine $1/3$ part sweet tea, $1/3$ part lemonade, $1/3$ part rum, fresh mint, and ice. Blend until well combined.
4. Pour into the sugar-rimmed glass. Serve with a lemon slice and sprig of mint.

Note: For a nonalcoholic version, mix equal parts iced tea and lemonade plus ice and mint.

6. Refrigerate for 3 hours.
7. To make the sour cream topping: In a small bowl, combine the sour cream, sugar, and vanilla and mix together.
8. Just before serving, top the pie with the sour cream topping.

HOT LITTLE TIP

Why So Low?

Using a low speed instead of high speed on the mixer for this cream cheese pie prevents air bubbles from forming that could cause cracks in the surface of the pie. So for a smooth surface, go nice and slow.

BEST EVER CHOCOLATE PIE

Someone reached out to me randomly on Instagram, someone I did not know. It turned out she had gone to college with my aunt, and she told me her family still made my grandfather's chocolate pie. I'd never heard of this recipe, and neither had my mother! My grandfather was one of the original health nuts, but he had a sweet tooth for chocolate, so it made complete sense that my grandmother would have made him this pie. It was so nice of my aunt's friend to reach out to us, and the recipe she passed along has come back to us as a no-longer-lost family tradition! Of course, I had to tweak it by adding double chocolate.

Makes 6 to 8 servings

Butter for greasing pie dish
4 ounces dark chocolate
4 ounces semisweet
    chocolate
1 1/2 tablespoons
    powdered sugar

3 tablespoons hot water
1 teaspoon vanilla extract
3 large egg whites
1/3 teaspoon salt
1/8 teaspoon cream of tartar

2 cups heavy whipping
    cream
1/2 cup sugar
1/2 cup chopped
    pecans, toasted

1. Preheat the oven to 300 degrees. Generously butter a pie dish and set aside.

2. In a double boiler over medium heat, combine the dark chocolate, semisweet chocolate, powdered sugar, hot water, and vanilla. Whisk until the chocolate has melted and is smooth. Remove the chocolate from the heat and let it cool slightly.

3. Using a stand mixer or hand mixer on medium-high speed, beat the egg whites until foamy to make a meringue. Add the salt and cream of tartar and continue to beat until stiff peaks form.

4. Slowly and gently fold half of the chocolate mixture into the meringue, reserving the remaining half of the chocolate mixture. This will take a few minutes—go slowly so you don't deflate the meringue. Once the chocolate and meringue are combined, pour it into the buttered pie dish. Bake for 30 minutes.

5. Remove the pie from the oven and let it cool completely.

6. While the pie is cooling, make the whipped cream. Using a stand mixer or hand mixer on medium-high speed, beat the heavy cream, gradually adding the sugar. Beat until the cream is shiny, and stiff peaks form.

7. Reserve half of the whipped cream and set it aside. With the remaining half of the whipped cream, slowly and gently fold in the remaining half of the chocolate mixture. You want the chocolate to be warm and not cold or it will seize up in the whipped cream. If the chocolate has completely cooled, put it back over the double boiler for a minute or in the microwave for a few seconds, then fold it into the cream. Stir until combined. Fold in the toasted pecans.

8. Top the cooled pie with the chocolate whipped cream and place it in the refrigerator for 2 to 3 hours to chill.

9. Serve with the remaining whipped cream.

SUMMER

For me, summer means freedom from cooking plans! It's all about losing track of time while we're enjoying our warm-weather adventures. For my summer recipes, I like dishes that I can either throw together in minutes or make ahead of time, so they're ready when we are. And if I can cook it outside, that's an added bonus. During the summer, I want to make food that can travel with us—on the boat, on a hike, or to a party—without having to think too hard about it, like cold or room-temperature salads that can sit. I love simple seafood dishes that come together quickly and meat that can marinate in the fridge until we're ready to toss it on the grill. For me, there's creativity in that carefree attitude toward cooking. It doesn't matter if we're eating around a campfire or we're still in our bathing suits. It doesn't matter what time it is. It's all about what easy, delicious dish we can make to keep the fun summer day going until it's time to turn in and then start all over again the next day.

WEEKNIGHT SUPPERS

Thai Chicken Salad

Lemon Zest Shrimp Salad

Herbed Pizza Crust Three Ways: Arugula, Parmesan, and Anchovy; Salami, Red Onions, and Capers; Carrie's Special

---

Linguini with Clams

Middle Eastern Chicken with Yogurt Shallot Sauce

Cheddar Jalapeño Corn Dogs

WEEKEND SUPPERS

Israeli Couscous and Scallops

Mediterranean Lamb Chops

Lemony Crab Pasta

Shrimp Toast

HOT LITTLE EXTRAS

Mint Snap Pea Salad

Butter Bean Hummus

Summer Succotash

Roasted Poblano Corn Salad

Herbed Fingerling Potatoes

Blue Cheese Roasted Onions

DRINKS AND DESSERTS

Pomegranate Margaritas

Briny Hounds

Killer Cookies

Rosé-Spiked Berry Crostata

WEEKNIGHT
SUPPERS

THAI CHICKEN SALAD

This is a perfect summer salad. It feeds a crowd, and it's one of those rare salads you can make ahead because it only tastes better after sitting awhile. The flavor from the vinaigrette satisfies my craving for Asian food, with the healthy benefits of a salad. Don't shy away from using fish sauce. It's a staple of Asian cooking that adds a depth of flavor. The smell you get in the bottle is not what presents in the dish. Give it a try!

Makes 6 to 8 servings

¼ cup vegetable oil

1 medium shallot, thinly sliced (about ¼ cup)

1 rotisserie chicken, meat removed and shredded (about 4 to 5 cups)

1 head purple cabbage, sliced paper thin (about 3 to 4 cups or 1 pound)

1 (8-ounce) package romaine hearts, chopped

2 red bell peppers, sliced into thin strips (about 2 cups)

1 cucumber, skin on, sliced into thin strips

1 cup matchstick carrots (1 large carrot)

4 green onions, chopped

½ cup peanuts

¼ cup fresh cilantro, chiffonade

¼ cup fresh basil, chiffonade

¼ cup fresh mint, chiffonade

Fresh jalapeño slices, for garnish (optional)

> **HOT LITTLE TIP**
>
> **Chiffonade**
>
> *Chiffonade:* a super-duper fancy word for "ribbons" in the cooking world! Stack, roll like a cigar, and chop away. Now aren't you fancy?

Soy Lime Vinaigrette

½ cup olive oil

6 tablespoons rice wine vinegar

2 tablespoons soy sauce

2 tablespoons toasted sesame oil

2 teaspoons fish sauce

2 tablespoons minced shallot

Zest and juice of 2 limes (about 2 teaspoons zest and about 3 to 4 tablespoons juice)

1. To make the soy lime vinaigrette: In a mason jar or other container, combine the olive oil, vinegar, soy sauce, sesame oil, fish sauce, shallot, lime zest, and lime juice. Top with a lid and shake until everything is mixed together.

2. In a small saucepan, heat the vegetable oil over medium-high heat. Once the oil reaches 350 degrees, carefully add the shallots, stirring until golden brown. Transfer the shallots immediately to paper towels to cool.

3. In a large bowl, combine the chicken, cabbage, romaine hearts, bell peppers,

cucumber, carrots, green onions, peanuts, cilantro, basil, and mint. Toss together. Add the vinaigrette and mix

well. Let the salad sit for 15 minutes before serving.

4. Top the salad with the fried shallots to serve.

Note: This is an easy weeknight salad, but it's also great to serve for a dinner party. If you want a smaller salad, halve the ingredients, but keep the same amount of chicken.

LEMON ZEST SHRIMP SALAD

At Callie's Hot Little Biscuit, our popular Wednesday special is shrimp and grits in a biscuit bowl. I get all the shrimp from the Tarvin and Magwood families on Shem Creek near my house, and when we have leftover shrimp from the special, I can't wait to take it home. It's too precious a delicacy to waste. This salad is one of my favorite ways to use shrimp, and it has become a summer staple at our house. You can serve it on its own, stuffed in a fluffy buttered biscuit, or on your favorite bread for an open-faced sandwich.

Makes 4 servings

2 pounds shrimp

3 celery stalks, chopped
(about 1 ½ cups)

Zest and juice of ½
lemon (about 1

teaspoon zest and 1 ½
tablespoons juice)

½ cup mayonnaise

2 green onions, chopped

2 tablespoons chopped
fresh dill

Salt and freshly ground
coarse black
pepper to taste

1. Bring 2 quarts of salted water to a boil. The water should taste salty. Add the shrimp and cook 2 to 3 minutes, until the shrimp turn pink. Drain the shrimp and place them in a bowl of ice water to stop the cooking. Peel and devein the shrimp. Cut each shrimp into thirds and place the pieces in a large bowl.

2. Add the celery, lemon zest, lemon juice, mayonnaise, green onions, dill, and salt and pepper. Stir until everything is well combined.

3. Cover and let the salad chill in the refrigerator for at least 30 minutes before serving.

HOT LITTLE TIP

To Devein or Not to Devein?

That is the question! My dad would never consider deveining, but Mom and I wouldn't dare eat a shrimp without! When I'm peeling shrimp, I take the time to devein using a small paring knife—I don't think any of the dedicated deveining gadgets out there work any better.

HERBED PIZZA CRUST THREE WAYS

Arugula, Parmesan, and Anchovy
Salami, Red Onions, and Capers
Carrie's Special

This pizza dough is surprisingly easy and comes together quickly. Since each batch makes enough dough for three pizzas, that means three blank canvases to be creative with. I love all of these flavors (particularly Carrie's Special!), but the topping possibilities are truly unlimited. Get everyone in the family involved in the kitchen, making their own creations, and see what will become the new family favorite! You can even do an outdoor pizza party and bake them in an Ooni pizza oven or on a Big Green Egg.

Makes 3 to 6 servings

PIZZA CRUST

1 ¼ cups warm water

1 packet active dry yeast

3 cups all-purpose flour

½ teaspoon sugar

1 teaspoon dried
    rosemary, minced

1 teaspoon dried oregano

1 teaspoon salt

½ teaspoon crushed
    red pepper flakes

3 tablespoons cornmeal,
    divided

ARUGULA PIZZA

3 tablespoons olive
    oil, divided

6 anchovies, finely diced

3 ounces arugula (about
    3 handfuls)

Juice of ½ lemon (1 to
    1 ½ tablespoons)

Freshly grated
    Parmesan cheese

Salt and freshly ground

coarse black
    pepper to taste

SALAMI PIZZA

1 tablespoon olive oil

¼ to ½ cup crushed
    tomatoes (or

homemade
    tomato sauce)

½ red onion, sliced
    (about ½ cup)

2 tablespoons capers

8 slices thinly sliced salami

½ to 1 cup freshly
    shredded mozzarella

CARRIE'S SPECIAL

1 tablespoon olive oil

¼ to ½ cup crushed
    tomatoes (or

homemade
    tomato sauce)

2 jalapeño peppers, sliced

thin (for less heat, you
    can remove the seeds)

½ to 1 cup freshly
    shredded mozzarella

1. To make the crust: In a small bowl, combine the warm water and yeast. Let it sit for 10 minutes. In a large bowl, combine the flour, sugar, rosemary, oregano, salt, and crushed red pepper flakes.

2. Slowly add the yeast and water to the dry ingredients, stirring to combine. If the mixture seems too dry, add a tablespoon of water at a time. The dough will be sticky.

3. Shape the dough into a ball and cover it with a damp cloth. Let it rest for 45 to 60 minutes. Then cut the dough into 3 equal portions.

4. Preheat the oven to 500 degrees. Heat a 12-inch cast-iron skillet in the oven for 30 minutes.

5. While the cast-iron skillet is heating, prepare the crust. Sprinkle 1 tablespoon of the cornmeal on a piece of parchment paper. Place one of the dough portions on top. Dust the top of the dough and the rolling pin with a little flour to prevent the rolling pin from sticking. Roll out the dough into a 10- to 12-inch circle ¼ inch thick. Repeat for the other two crusts.

6. To make the arugula pizza: Brush the hot cast-iron skillet with 1 tablespoon of the olive oil. Place the rolled-out dough in the skillet. Brush the top of the dough with another tablespoon of olive oil. Sprinkle the chopped anchovies on top. Bake for 10 to 15 minutes, or until the crust is crisp and golden brown. While the crust is baking, in a large bowl, toss together the arugula, lemon juice, Parmesan, remaining tablespoon of olive oil, and salt and pepper. When the crust is finished baking, remove it from the skillet and place it on a cutting board or serving platter. Top the pizza with the arugula mixture and some more grated Parmesan and serve immediately.

7. To make the salami pizza: Brush the hot cast-iron skillet with the olive oil. Place the rolled-out dough in the skillet. Top with the crushed tomatoes, onions, capers, salami, and mozzarella. Bake for 10 to 12 minutes, or until the cheese is melted and the crust is golden brown. Remove the pizza from the oven and serve immediately.

8. To make Carrie's Special: Brush the hot cast-iron skillet with the olive oil. Place the rolled-out dough in the skillet. Top with the crushed tomatoes, sliced jalapeños, and mozzarella. Bake for 10 to 12 minutes, or until the cheese is melted and the crust is golden brown. Remove the pizza from the oven and serve immediately.

HOT LITTLE TIP

Best Pizza Mozza

When we're making pizza, I put fresh mozzarella in the blender or food processor and pulse for a few seconds. Then I place the shredded cheese in between two clean kitchen towels to let it dry for a few minutes before using it.

HOT LITTLE TIP

Pizza on the Patio: Big Green Eggs and Ooni Ovens

To cook your pizza on a Big Green Egg, it's best to have the indirect heat element, a pizza stone, and a wooden pizza peel. Start your fire and put the indirect heat element on. Get the fire really hot, until at least a fourth of the charcoal is white. Put the pizza stone on top of the indirect element for at least 10 minutes. Sprinkle semolina or cornmeal onto the pizza peel. Add the rolled-out pizza crust dough to the peel, then assemble all of the ingredients on top of the dough. Slide the pizza onto the hot stone. Put the hood of the grill down and cook the pizza for 10 to 15 minutes, checking it for your desired amount of char.

If you're really a pizza fan, invest in an Ooni Pro outdoor pizza oven. It's portable, it has a fast bake time, it's easy to use, and it makes the best crispy crust!

LINGUINI WITH CLAMS

Caroline came home one day after spending the night with a friend, raving about the linguini with clams they'd eaten. As always, I had to try it myself! This is a simple summer pasta. In my experience, when you'd like to expose children to foods they wouldn't normally go for, like clams, if you add it to pasta, they will eat it up. John likes to make homemade pasta. I shy away from it because of the mess and also because I love the fresh pasta bar at Whole Foods. It makes life a little easier.

Makes 4 to 6 servings

- 1 (4-ounce) package chopped pancetta
- 1 tablespoon olive oil
- 1 white onion, diced (about 1 cup)
- 10 cloves garlic, minced (about 3 tablespoons)
- 2 ½ pounds fresh clams (whatever size is available and freshest)
- 1 cup dry white wine
- 1 pound fresh black pepper linguini (or any linguini)
- 3 tablespoons salted butter
- Juice of 2 lemons (4 to 6 tablespoons)
- 2 cups arugula (about 2 handfuls)
- 1 cup reserved pasta water
- ½ cup chopped fresh flat-leaf Italian parsley

1. Bring a large pot of salted water to a boil.
2. Heat a large, heavy skillet over medium heat. Add the pancetta and cook until crisp. Remove the pancetta from the skillet and drain on paper towels.
3. In the same skillet, add the olive oil to the pancetta grease. Add the onions and sauté over medium heat until the onions soften, about 5 minutes. Add the garlic and cook for another 2 minutes, stirring frequently.
4. Add the clams and wine to the skillet with the onions and garlic. Put a lid on the skillet and cook the clams for 6 to 8 minutes, or until the clams have opened. Discard any unopened clams.
5. While the clams are cooking, add the pasta to the boiling water. Cook the pasta according to the package directions for al dente.
6. Drain the pasta, reserving and setting aside 1 cup of the pasta water.
7. Add the butter to the empty pasta pot. Return the drained pasta to the pot. Add the lemon juice and mix to combine. Turn the heat to low.
8. Add the cooked pancetta and arugula to the pasta and mix until combined. Add a little of the pasta water to help thicken the sauce.
9. Once the clams finish cooking, remove the clams from the skillet and set aside. Add the entire contents of the skillet to the pasta and mix together. Divide the pasta among warmed serving bowls and top with the clams.
10. Garnish with the fresh parsley and serve immediately.

HOT LITTLE TIP

Get Creative and Don't Be Afraid to Make Substitutions

What's the worst that can happen? You can't find clams, but you've got shrimp. You wanted snapper, but the only thing fresh was flounder. The recipe calls for chicken thighs, but you have breasts. The grocery store is out of limes but has plenty of grapefruit. Cooking isn't like baking, where it's an exact science. Use what you have on hand and see how it goes. You might even create a new favorite! Have fun experimenting with different ingredients, whether it's by design or necessity.

MIDDLE EASTERN CHICKEN WITH YOGURT SHALLOT SAUCE

This is inspired by a recipe my sister-in-law Meghan makes. She has a fantastic kitchen, and when we're in Idaho in the summer, we always go over to her house to sample whatever delicious recipe she's most recently discovered. This particular dish blew me away, so I had to make my own version. The texture of the chicken thighs, with the crunchy vegetable salad and flatbread on the side, makes the perfect summer supper.

Makes 4 servings

4 cloves garlic, minced
(about 4 teaspoons)
½ white onion, diced
(about ½ cup)
Juice of 1 lemon (about
2 to 3 tablespoons)
4 to 5 tablespoons olive oil
1 tablespoon turmeric
1 tablespoon cumin
1 tablespoon coriander
1 teaspoon garam masala
1 teaspoon chili powder

1 teaspoon paprika
1 teaspoon allspice
1 teaspoon ground ginger
½ teaspoon cayenne
pepper
1 ½ pounds boneless,
skinless chicken thighs
1 large cucumber, diced
1 pint mixed medley of
cherry tomatoes
½ red onion, diced
(about ½ cup)

1 red bell pepper, diced
(about 1 cup)
1 yellow bell pepper,
diced (about 1 cup)
3 to 4 tablespoons
lemon vinaigrette
Salt and freshly ground
coarse black
pepper to taste
Flatbread to serve

YOGURT SHALLOT SAUCE

1 cup plain Greek yogurt
½ medium-size shallot,
minced (about ¼ cup)

2 tablespoons olive
oil, divided
Salt and freshly ground

coarse black
pepper to taste

LEMON VINAIGRETTE

2 tablespoons Dijon
mustard
1 clove garlic, minced
(about 1 teaspoon)

1 teaspoon minced onion
Juice of ½ lemon (1 to
2 tablespoons)
¼ cup white wine vinegar

1 cup olive oil
Salt and freshly ground
coarse black
pepper to taste

1. To make the sauce: In a small bowl, combine the yogurt, shallot, 1 tablespoon of olive oil, and salt and pepper. Let it sit on the counter to allow the flavors to meld.

2. To make the vinaigrette: In a mason

or 2 corn dogs at a time. Let the corn dogs sink to the bottom of the pot and turn them with tongs so that they cook evenly on all sides and turn golden brown, about 2 to 3 minutes. As they finish, transfer the corn dogs to the wire rack in the oven to stay warm and crisp until they're all fried.

Note: I love to serve these in plastic baskets lined with parchment paper.

HOT LITTLE TIP

Hot Little Puppies

You can always forgo the corn dog sticks. Cut the hot dogs in thirds before battering and make corn pups instead!

HOT LITTLE TIPS

Cooking Outside

We love to cook outside! Outside the RV in Idaho, our makeshift kitchen includes a mop sink, propane grill, and a small smoker. Anyone can set up to cook outside. If you're frying, it cuts down on the smell and the mess inside the house. And it's just more fun to cook in the open summer air. If you have a propane burner, you can pretty much cook anything outside that you can cook inside on the stove.

Here are some ideas of equipment and tools for setting up an outdoor cooking station:

- Propane tank with a burner and/or grill
- Big Dutch oven for frying and cooking stews and chilis
- Large pot with insert to cook corn on the cob, shrimp, or a Lowcountry boil
- Deep-fry thermometer, so you can keep an eye on the temperature when frying
- Wire rack on a rimmed baking sheet
- Tongs and/or a bamboo skimmer
- My Traveling Kitchen Kit: I don't go anywhere without it! My chef's knife, Messermeister vegetable peeler, garlic press, zester, mandoline slicer, instant-read thermometer, and long lighter, all wrapped in kitchen towels.

WEEKEND
SUPPERS

ISRAELI COUSCOUS AND SCALLOPS

It doesn't matter who it is—everybody loves this dish. People tell me this is their favorite thing that I make. It's simple enough for a weeknight but especially perfect for a weekend dinner party. The flavor profile is intense yet light at the same time—just right for summer!

Makes 4 servings   (W)

2 cups halved mixed medley of cherry tomatoes

½ onion, diced (about ¼ cup)

2 cloves garlic, minced (about 2 teaspoons)

3 tablespoons olive oil

Salt and freshly ground coarse black pepper to taste

1 ⅓ cups Israeli couscous (if it's flavored, discard the seasoning packet)

2 ¾ cups vegetable broth

3 tablespoons bacon grease (or vegetable oil)

12 large sea scallops, rinsed and dried completely on paper towels and small side muscle removed

2 cups arugula

¼ cup lemon vinaigrette

⅓ cup chopped fresh flat-leaf Italian parsley

⅓ cup pine nuts, toasted

2 green onions, diced

Zest of 1 lemon (about 2 teaspoons)

Pinch of crushed red pepper flakes

> ## HOT LITTLE TIP
>
> ### Try Israeli Couscous
>
> The Israeli or "pearl" variety of couscous is larger than regular couscous. It is a beautiful blank canvas for all your creations. It can be served hot or cold, similar to orzo. You can toss in any herb or veggie for a side dish or top it with a protein. Don't pass it by in the grocery aisle—give it a try and elevate your hot little suppers.

LEMON VINAIGRETTE

2 tablespoons Dijon mustard

1 clove garlic, minced (about 1 teaspoon)

1 teaspoon minced onion

Juice of ½ lemon (1 to 2 tablespoons)

¼ cup white wine vinegar

1 cup olive oil

Salt and freshly ground coarse black pepper to taste

1. To make the vinaigrette: In a mason jar or other container, combine the mustard, garlic, onions, lemon juice, vinegar, olive oil, and salt and pepper. Top with a lid and shake until everything is mixed together. Keep refrigerated until ready to use. This recipe makes a generous cup. Enjoy the remainder with seafood salads, chicken salad, or over grilled vegetables like broccoli, asparagus, and artichokes.

2. Preheat the oven to 425 degrees. Line a rimmed baking sheet with parchment paper.

3. In a large bowl, combine the tomatoes, onions, garlic, olive oil, and salt and pepper. Pour the mixture onto the parchment-lined baking sheet. Bake for 12 to 15 minutes. Set aside to cool.

4. Heat a Dutch oven or medium saucepan over medium heat. Add the couscous and toast for 5 minutes, stirring occasionally.

5. Slowly add the vegetable broth to the couscous. Stir until combined. Bring it to a boil, then reduce the heat to a simmer. Cover. Stir frequently, making sure the couscous doesn't burn or stick to the bottom of the pan. Simmer until the liquid has absorbed and the couscous is tender. Remove the pot from the heat and let it cool. If any liquid remains, drain it.

6. Heat a cast-iron skillet or sauté pan over medium-high heat. Let the pan get screaming hot! Add the bacon grease. Pat the scallops dry one more time. Then, working in two batches so you don't overcrowd the pan, add the scallops to the pan. Cook for 2 to 3 minutes per side. Do not touch the scallops until it is time to flip them. You can place a sheet of foil over the pan, so grease doesn't splatter everywhere. To test for doneness, touch the scallops, which should bounce back slightly. Once they are done, remove the skillet from the heat and set them aside.

7. In a large bowl or platter, combine the couscous, roasted tomato mixture, and arugula. Stir in the lemon vinaigrette. Add the parsley, pine nuts, green onions, lemon zest, crushed red pepper, and salt and pepper. Top with the scallops and serve.

Note: I recommend Kitchen Basics brand vegetable stock.

MEDITERRANEAN LAMB CHOPS

I love everything about lamb chops, down to sucking on the bone to find those last hidden bits of flavorful fat. These chops are so quick and easy to prepare, yet I always feel fancy when I serve them. They are expensive, though, and I always want more! These will make you a rock star with your guests, and they pair beautifully with Israeli couscous and my Yogurt Shallot Sauce (page 75).

Makes 4 to 6 servings

8 to 12 lamb chops

Salt and freshly ground

coarse black

pepper to taste

I tablespoon olive oil

TAPENADE

½ pound mixed
olives, pitted

3 to 4 anchovies, rinsed

2 cloves garlic

I teaspoon lemon zest

I cup fresh flat-leaf
Italian parsley

I tablespoon capers (rinsed
if packed in salt)

¼ red onion, diced
(about ¼ cup)

I tablespoon olive oil

1. Take the lamb chops out of the refrigerator at least 30 minutes before cooking (or until they are room temperature) and season liberally with salt and pepper.

2. To make the tapenade: In a food processor or blender, combine the olives, anchovies, garlic, lemon zest, parsley, capers, red onions, and olive oil. Pulse until the mixture forms a smooth paste.

3. Reserve ¼ cup of the tapenade and rub the remainder over both sides of the lamb chops.

4. In a large cast-iron skillet, heat the olive oil over medium-high heat. Once the pan is smoking hot, sear each side for 3 to 4 minutes per side for medium rare. Cook longer, if needed, to reach your desired temperature.

5. Remove the lamb chops from the pan and let them rest for 10 minutes. Top with the reserved tapenade and serve.

LEMONY CRAB PASTA

This recipe is inspired by one of my favorite dishes at FIG in Charleston. As luscious as my version is, it doesn't even begin to do the original justice. This dish is light, bright, and takes a little bit of crab a long way. Throw a white tablecloth on your table, and this unexpected pasta can almost transport you to a summer evening at FIG.

Makes 4 to 6 servings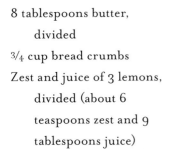

8 tablespoons butter, divided
3/4 cup bread crumbs
Zest and juice of 3 lemons, divided (about 6 teaspoons zest and 9 tablespoons juice)

1 pound fettuccine or linguini
2 tablespoons olive oil
1/2 white onion, diced (about 1/2 cup)
3 cloves garlic, minced (about 3 teaspoons)

1 pound lump crabmeat
1 cup reserved pasta water
1 teaspoon crushed red pepper flakes (or more if you like spice)
1/4 cup thinly sliced fresh mint

1. Heat a sauté pan over medium-high heat and add 2 tablespoons of the butter. Add the bread crumbs and stir to combine. Toast the bread crumbs for 3 to 5 minutes, stirring occasionally, being careful not to burn the crumbs. Remove them from the heat and add 1 tablespoon of the lemon zest to the pan. Stir to combine.

2. In a large pot, cook the pasta according to the package directions. Drain the pasta, reserving 1 cup of the pasta water.

3. Heat a large, heavy skillet over medium heat. Add the olive oil and 2 tablespoons of the butter. Add the onions and sauté until the onions are softened, about 5 minutes. Add the garlic and cook another minute. Add the crabmeat and cook for 5 minutes. Add 1/4 cup of the reserved pasta water and stir to combine.

4. Add the cooked pasta to the skillet with the crab. Stir to combine. Add the remaining 4 tablespoons of butter, crushed red pepper, lemon juice, and remaining zest. Stir to combine, adding more pasta water if needed to thicken the sauce. The sauce should thicken slightly, and the pasta should look shiny.

5. Top with the lemony bread crumbs and fresh mint and serve immediately.

SHRIMP TOAST

Here's my ideal scenario of summer entertaining with friends. Spend the day on the boat. Go for a dip in the pool. Make a pitcher of margaritas. Ride bikes to Abundant Seafood on Shem Creek. Get royal red shrimp. Make some toast. Throw the shrimp on the grill and douse it in hot garlic butter. Pour it over the toast on a huge platter. Have everyone gather around and eat with their fingers. Shrimp Toast is my favorite on-the-fly summer supper. Other than the fresh shrimp, you're using what you already have. You don't even need plates or utensils. It's a no-plan, no-fuss, don't-have-to-sit-at-the-table, interactive meal to cap the perfect summer day.

HOT LITTLE TIP

Try Royal Reds

Royal red shrimp are special. They're bigger than other varieties of shrimp and have a rich, robust taste, almost like lobster. They need little seasoning because they already pack a salty, buttery punch. The peak season for royal reds is late summer. Fresh is always best, but you can find these frozen year-round. At the market, go for the smaller shrimp. They tend to be sweeter and more delicious. Ask your fishmonger when they're coming in and be ready to develop a new summertime craving!

Makes 8 to 10 servings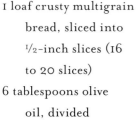

1 loaf crusty multigrain bread, sliced into ½-inch slices (16 to 20 slices)

6 tablespoons olive oil, divided

12 cloves garlic, 2 whole and 10 minced

3 pounds royal red shrimp, peeled and deveined (can substitute large or extra-large regular shrimp)

1 cup (2 sticks) butter

Zest and juice of 2 lemons, divided (about 4 teaspoons zest and 6 tablespoons juice)

½ cup chopped fresh flat-leaf Italian parsley

Maldon sea salt for finishing

Freshly ground coarse black pepper to taste

Crushed red pepper flakes to taste

1. Heat the grill to high heat.
2. Brush each slice of bread using 4 tablespoons of the olive oil and place them on the hot grill. Cook on each side for 1 minute or less, until crisp and toasted. Remove the bread from the heat and place it on a large platter. Rub the whole cloves of garlic all over the grilled bread.
3. In a large bowl, add the shrimp, drizzle the remaining 2 tablespoons of olive oil

over the shrimp, and toss to coat. Place the shrimp on the hot grill and cook for 1 to 2 minutes on each side, or until the shrimp are cooked through, being careful not to overcook them.

4. Remove the shrimp from the grill and place them in another large bowl.

5. In a small saucepan over medium heat, combine the butter, lemon zest, minced garlic, and parsley. Simmer for 5 minutes, then stir in the lemon juice and remove the pot from the heat. Taste for salt and lemon and adjust to your taste.

6. Pour the butter mixture over the shrimp and toss to combine.

7. Pour the coated shrimp over the toasted bread on the platter.

8. Season with the sea salt, pepper, and crushed red pepper flakes and serve.

HOT
LITTLE
EXTRAS

MINT SNAP PEA SALAD

When I was in New York City for the Fancy Food Show, my mother and I ate our final meal of the trip at Café Altro Paradiso. I was excited about all the pasta, but the server insisted we try the mint snap pea salad. He was raving about it, so we ordered it to see what the fuss was about. He did not steer us wrong. It was seriously one of the best things I've ever put in my mouth—bursting with super-fresh flavor. Ever since, I have been on a tear creating my own version, over and over and over again. I can't get enough!

Makes 2 to 4 servings

3 cups fresh snap peas

1 tablespoon olive oil

3 tablespoons fresh bread crumbs, pine nuts, or chopped almonds

½ red onion, sliced paper thin

2 radishes, cut into thin matchsticks

1 tablespoon fresh mint, chiffonade

Juice of 1 lime (1 ½ to 2 tablespoons juice)

Zest of 1 lemon (about 2 teaspoons)

2 tablespoons shaved Parmesan cheese

2 tablespoons shaved Havarti cheese

Salt and freshly ground coarse black pepper to taste

1. Fill a large pot with water and bring it to a boil. Add the snap peas and boil for 2 minutes. Drain the peas and cover them with ice to keep them from continuing to cook. Once they have cooled, drain the water.

2. Heat a skillet over medium heat. Add the olive oil. Add the bread crumbs (or pine nuts or almonds) and stir until toasted. Once the bread crumbs are toasted, remove the skillet from the heat and let them cool completely.

3. In a large serving bowl, combine the snap peas, red onions, radishes, mint, lime juice, lemon zest, Parmesan, Havarti, and salt and pepper. Top with the toasted bread crumbs to serve.

BUTTER BEAN HUMMUS

Growing up with my dad, we kept suppers simple, which often meant butter beans over rice with salt and pepper. I'd be happy to have that as my last meal on earth. I made this variation on butter beans for an event at the Cigar Factory, a large, iconic building in Charleston. This was before it had been renovated, and there was no electricity except for a few extension cords, no lighting other than candles and string lights, and no air-conditioning—in August! I was wearing a cute silk summer dress and high heels, and I had brought my friend Amanda with me. Since my dish was make-ahead, I went to the kitchen area to help serve so the other cooks and chefs could keep working. I tripped on something, and butter bean hummus flew everywhere—all over me, my dress, and the floor. By the time I got cleaned up and back to the table, Amanda had passed out from the heat. I have to laugh when I think about butter bean hummus and that hot, fun, chaotic memory—my life in a butter bean shell!

Makes 4 to 6 servings

2 cups butter beans
(or lima beans)

Reserved strained
liquid from beans

3 cloves garlic

1 teaspoon cumin

1/2 teaspoon paprika

3 green onions, chopped

Juice of 1 lemon (about
3 tablespoons)

1/4 cup fresh cilantro

1/4 teaspoon cayenne
pepper (optional
for added heat)

Salt and freshly ground
coarse black
pepper to taste

2 tablespoons finely
minced red onion

2 tablespoons olive oil

2 tablespoons chopped
fresh mint

1 teaspoon chopped
fresh dill

1. In a medium saucepan over medium heat, combine the butter beans and just enough water to cover them. Simmer for 30 minutes. Once the beans are tender, remove the pot from the heat and strain the liquid from the beans, reserving the strained liquid.

2. In a food processor, combine the garlic, cumin, paprika, green onions, lemon juice, cilantro, and cayenne pepper if using. Pulse until combined.

3. Add all but 1/4 cup of the butter beans to the food processor and pulse to combine. Slowly add the reserved butter bean liquid until it gets to your desired consistency. Add the salt and pepper.

4. Scoop the hummus into a serving bowl. Garnish with the remaining 1/4 cup butter beans, red onions, olive oil, mint, and dill to serve.

Note: You can use frozen butter beans or lima beans if you can't find fresh.

SUMMER SUCCOTASH

This dish celebrates all the beautiful colors of summer and roadside produce-stand vegetables. It's so versatile—you can serve it hot or cold, topped with a protein, or as a side. Add a tomato slice and it's a meal all its own.

Makes 4 servings

1 cup butter beans
Salt and freshly ground
    coarse black
      pepper to taste
1 tablespoon olive oil

2 tablespoons butter,
    divided
1 cup okra (cut into
    $^1/_4$-inch pieces,
    about $^1/_4$ pound)

1 white onion, diced
    (about 1 cup)
1 cup raw corn, cut off
    the cob (about 2
    medium ears)
$^1/_4$ cup white wine

1. In a medium saucepan over medium heat, combine the butter beans and just enough water to cover them. Add a pinch of salt. Simmer for 30 minutes. Once the beans are tender, remove the pot from the heat and strain the liquid from the beans.

2. In a cast-iron skillet over medium-high heat, combine the olive oil and 1 tablespoon of the butter. Add the okra and onions and cook until slightly brown, 6 to 8 minutes, making sure not to overstir.

3. Reduce the heat to medium and add the butter beans. Cook for another 5 minutes.

4. Add the corn and salt and pepper. Stir to combine. Add the wine and toss to coat. Cook for 1 to 2 minutes to reduce the liquids, then remove the skillet from the heat.

5. Add the remaining tablespoon of butter, tossing to coat. Serve immediately.

HOT LITTLE TIP

Mix Up Your Veggies

Succotash can be any combination of veggies. If you don't like or have okra, substitute tomatoes, frozen peas, or whatever you have!

ROASTED POBLANO CORN SALAD

I've always been a corn salad fan, and this is one of my reinventions of it. The smoky taste of the roasted poblanos elevates the corn to a whole new level. This is a great salad to make ahead and take to a summer get-together or picnic.

Makes 10 servings

5 poblano peppers

8 to 10 fresh ears of corn, shucked

2 red bell peppers, diced (about 2 cups)

4 green onions, diced

5 ounces arugula

½ cup roasted pepitas (pumpkin seeds)

½ cup Cotija cheese (or feta)

¼ cup olive oil

Juice of ½ lime (½ to 1 tablespoon)

Salt and freshly ground coarse black pepper to taste

1. To roast the poblanos: Using tongs, hold the peppers right over the open flame of a gas stove burner. Turn them as they get black. If you don't have a gas stove, put the peppers on a rimmed baking sheet and broil them in the oven. Once they cool, remove the bubbled (blistered) skin. Cut the peppers open, remove the seeds, and chop.

2. Bring a large pot of water to a boil. Once the water is boiling, carefully add the ears of corn. Boil for 1 minute. Then turn off the heat and cover the pot. Let it stand for 30 minutes.

3. Cut the corn off the cob and add it to a large bowl. It should yield about 5 cups of corn.

4. Add the poblanos, bell peppers, green onions, arugula, pepitas, Cotija, olive oil, and lime juice to the corn. Toss to combine and taste for salt and pepper. Serve immediately or keep in the fridge until ready to serve.

HERBED FINGERLING POTATOES

This is my version of an updated potato salad, without the mayo overload. What I love about fingerling potatoes is how they come in so many different sizes, shapes, and colors, which makes them visually appealing and interesting. The key to success with this recipe is using one of the big stainless steel bowls I mentioned in the biscuit chapter and having it out and prepped for when the potatoes come out of the oven. You want the potatoes hot when you coat them in the herbs. This dish tastes even better the next day.

Makes 4 to 6 servings

1 pound fingerling potatoes

4 tablespoons olive oil, divided

1/4 cup mayonnaise

2 tablespoons chopped fresh thyme, divided

2 tablespoons chopped fresh basil, divided

2 tablespoons chopped fresh flat-leaf Italian parsley, divided

2 green onions, chopped

1 clove garlic, minced (about 1 teaspoon)

Salt and freshly ground coarse black pepper to taste

1. Preheat the oven to 425 degrees. Line a rimmed baking sheet with parchment paper.

2. Cut the potatoes in half lengthwise, then place them on the baking sheet. Toss them with 1 tablespoon of the olive oil. Roast the potatoes for 25 to 30 minutes, or until golden brown and fork tender.

3. While the potatoes are roasting, in a large bowl combine the mayonnaise with 1 tablespoon of the thyme, 1 tablespoon of the basil, and 1 tablespoon of the parsley. Add the green onions, garlic, and the remaining 3 tablespoons of olive oil. Mix well, then smear it around the sides of the bowl.

4. Add the roasted potatoes, hot and right out of the oven, to the bowl and toss them very well until coated. Add salt and pepper to taste. Top with the remaining tablespoons of thyme, basil, and parsley. Serve hot, cold, or at room temperature.

HOT LITTLE TIP

Season Seasonally

For this potato salad, you can switch out the herbs based on the season or availability. For example, in cooler months when basil is scarce, try rosemary instead. If it's spring, consider dill. Use whatever fresh herbs you have on hand and discover your favorite flavor combinations.

BLUE CHEESE ROASTED ONIONS

A friend in Idaho had us over for steaks, and when she told me about these onions she was making, I thought to myself that it would never work. She proved me wrong. This dish is the new baked potato at my house. It's the perfect side or topping for steaks and burgers. What it lacks in visual beauty it makes up for many times over in taste. Soft butter plus blue cheese plus caramelized onions—yum! Don't doubt it. Try it!

Makes 4 servings

5 ounces blue cheese or Gorgonzola

3 tablespoons butter, softened

1 teaspoon Worcestershire sauce

1 clove garlic, minced (1 teaspoon)

1 large Vidalia onion (about 12 ounces), thickly sliced into 4 or 5 slices

1. Preheat the oven to 425 degrees.
2. In a small bowl, combine the blue cheese, butter, Worcestershire, and garlic.
3. Top the onion slices with the blue cheese mixture, about 1 1/2 tablespoons per onion slice.
4. Place the onion slices in a glass baking dish. Roast for 20 to 25 minutes, or until golden brown and bubbly.
5. Serve as a side dish or on top of a juicy steak or hamburger.

DRINKS
AND
DESSERTS

POMEGRANATE MARGARITAS

When John and I were dating, I was living in New York. We had a whirlwind romance, and after only three months, he sent me on a scavenger hunt around the city to our favorite places. One stop was Rosa Mexicano. There, our favorite bartender made me our regular—a pomegranate margarita. As he handed me my drink, he also passed along a note with the last clue of the hunt, the one that led me to John, who was waiting on one knee to propose. I have yet to tire of pomegranate margaritas—or John!

Makes 4 to 6 cocktails

1/2 cup pomegranate juice

1/2 cup fresh lime juice

1/2 to 3/4 cup simple syrup,

depending on how
sweet you like it

1 cup blanco tequila

Ice

1 lime, cut into wedges

SUGAR RIM

2 tablespoons
turbinado sugar

1 tablespoon salt

Zest of 1 lime plus 1

lime wedge (about
1 teaspoon zest)

SIMPLE SYRUP

1 cup sugar

1 cup water

1. To make the simple syrup: In a small saucepan over medium heat, combine the sugar and water. Bring the mixture to a low boil. Stir until the sugar dissolves. Turn off the heat, and let it cool completely.

2. To make the sugar rim: In a small bowl, combine the turbinado sugar, salt, and lime zest. Run the lime wedge over the rim of the glasses. Dip each rim into the sugar mixture and roll to cover.

3. In a blender, combine the pomegranate

juice, lime juice, simple syrup, and tequila. Add ice and blend until thoroughly combined.

4. Pour the margaritas into the sugar-rimmed glasses. Garnish with a fresh lime wedge.

Note: You can juice a whole pomegranate in your electric juicer, and it will yield about 1/2 cup juice. If you don't have a juicer, you can use store-bought pomegranate juice.

HOT LITTLE TIP

Take the Party with You

Instead of serving immediately, leave the margaritas, or whatever frozen drinks you're making, in the blender with the lid on. Place the blender jar in a cooler with ice, and take it out on the boat or to the pool!

BRINY HOUNDS

My grandmother Caroline loved a cocktail. I can still hear her long Southern drawl: "I'll have a saahlty dog." This take on the classic salty dog is a bit lighter than the original, with the addition of soda water and mint. It looks so pretty with the color of the grapefruit juice and the bubbles from the soda. It's light and refreshing—perfect for a summer day.

Makes 1 cocktail

Ice

1/3 cup freshly squeezed grapefruit juice

1/8 cup freshly squeezed lemon juice

1 1/2 ounces vodka

1 tablespoon mint simple syrup

1/3 cup soda water

Grapefruit slices

SWEET AND SPICY RIM

4 tablespoons sugar

2 teaspoons kosher salt

1 teaspoon smoked paprika

1/4 teaspoon cayenne pepper

1 lime wedge

MINT SIMPLE SYRUP

1 cup sugar

1 cup water

1/2 cup torn mint leaves

Zest of 1/2 lime (about

1/2 teaspoon)

1. To make the mint simple syrup: In a small saucepan over medium heat, combine the sugar, water, mint leaves, and lime zest. Bring the mixture to a low boil. Stir until the sugar dissolves. Turn off the heat, and let it cool completely. Strain. Store the syrup in a glass jar in the refrigerator for up to 3 weeks.

2. To make the sweet and spicy rim: In a small bowl, combine the sugar, salt, paprika, and cayenne. Run the lime wedge over the rim of a glass. Dip the rim into the sweet and spicy mix and roll to cover.

3. Fill a cocktail shaker with ice. Add the grapefruit juice, lemon juice, vodka, and mint simple syrup. Put the lid on and shake for 30 seconds, or until the ingredients have chilled.

4. Add ice to the glass with the sweet and spicy rim. Pour the cocktail over the ice, straining it with the shaker. Add the soda water and garnish with grapefruit slices.

KILLER COOKIES

Our family friend GoGo is one of those people who has a huge personality and lives life to the fullest. She lives in Laramie, Wyoming, and when we're out West, my girls love to visit with her. They go straight to her closet and dress up in her exotic clothes and hairpieces from her travels all over the world. She loves to entertain . . . cooking, not so much. She hosts plenty of parties, but there's no food in her house or plans for dinner. But she does keep cookies in her freezer for hungry visitors. This recipe is a great one to keep in your own freezer for a quick, cold treat all summer long.

Makes 10 to 12 cookies

10 ounces graham crackers (2 sleeves)

1 cup (2 sticks) butter

⅓ cup sugar

2 ounces chocolate chips, melted

1 cup crushed pecans

1. Line a rimmed baking sheet with parchment paper.

2. Arrange the graham crackers in a single layer on top of the parchment paper, covering the whole baking sheet.

3. In a sauté pan, melt the butter and sugar. Whisk constantly until bubbly and foam rises in the pan.

4. Pour the butter mixture over the graham crackers, then spread it with a spatula, making sure to cover all of the crackers.

5. Using a spoon, drizzle the melted chocolate over the graham crackers, then sprinkle the crushed pecans on top.

6. Freeze for at least 1 hour.

7. Remove the cookies from the freezer and break them into pieces. Store leftovers in the freezer.

Note: I prefer dark chocolate, but you can use any variety. And I recommend using Callie's Hot Little Biscuit Cocktail Pecans, which are especially salty and buttery.

ROSÉ-SPIKED BERRY CROSTATA

This recipe combines beautiful Fourth of July–themed colors with rosé wine, which had just hit the summer party scene when I first made this and continues to be popular. My mother-in-law always makes our wonderful meal for the Fourth and I bring dessert, so it's always a chance for me to experiment with red, white, and blue sweets!

Makes 6 to 8 servings

2 cups self-rising flour

1/3 cup plus 2 tablespoons white sugar, divided

10 tablespoons salted butter, divided (8 tablespoons at room temperature and 2 tablespoons melted)

1/3 cup plus 2 tablespoons whole milk

1 teaspoon vanilla extract

6 ounces fresh blackberries

16 ounces fresh strawberries, sliced

1/3 cup rosé

3 tablespoons turbinado sugar

Vanilla ice cream to serve

1. Preheat the oven to 350 degrees. Line a rimmed baking sheet with parchment paper.

2. In a large bowl, combine the flour, 1/3 cup of the white sugar, and the 8 tablespoons of room-temperature butter. Mix together quickly, working the mixture with your hands until it resembles coarse crumbs.

3. In a small bowl, combine the milk and vanilla. Add it to the flour mixture and mix it together with your hands. If the mixture seems too dry, add another tablespoon of milk. Work the dough into a ball. Wrap the dough in plastic wrap and refrigerate for 30 minutes.

4. While the dough is chilling, macerate the berries. In a small bowl, combine the blackberries, strawberries, rosé, and the remaining 2 tablespoons of white sugar. Let the berries sit for 30 minutes.

5. Lightly flour a working surface. Pinch off a small piece of dough about the size of a golf ball and set it aside. Roll out the rest of the dough into a rough square 10 to 12 inches across and 1/8 inch thick.

6. Roll out the small piece of reserved dough into a 1/8-inch thick rectangle. Using a pasta cutter or knife, cut it into 3 ribbons lengthwise and set them aside.

7. Carefully transfer the square of dough onto the parchment-lined baking sheet.

8. Drain the berries. To create an American flag design, place the blackberries in the upper left corner of the dough square. Then place the sliced strawberries on the rest of the dough, leaving about an inch or so around the edge.

9. Gently fold the edges of the dough up over the berries, pinching together any open seams. Add the 3 reserved ribbons of dough across the exposed berries to resemble the stripes of the flag. Brush the 2 tablespoons of melted butter all over the dough and sprinkle with the turbinado sugar.

10. Bake for 30 to 35 minutes, or until the dough is golden brown. Serve with vanilla ice cream.

Note: I recommend Hogwash rosé.

HOT LITTLE TIP

Crostata Crust Options

You can use any piecrust recipe for this crostata. Or save some time and use a store-bought piecrust. Roll it out the same way and reserve a pinch of dough to make the ribbons for the stripes on the flag. It's summertime, and this recipe is adaptable, so do whatever is most fun and most convenient for you!

FALL

Fall is all about getting back into a routine after summer's unstructured, no-rules spirit. I strategically plan out our weeknight suppers around school activities, practices, and games. One-pot meals, sandwiches, and quick fixes become the weekly norm, but on the weekends I like to pour myself a glass of wine and think about who we want to have over for supper. After the organized chaos of the week, it's time for me to unwind and enjoy some adult company.

Soups are a supremely simple and tasty way to feed a crowd. On the other hand, if I'm making something fancier that takes more attention, I don't mind standing in the kitchen over a hot stove, as long as friends and cocktails keep me company! It's nice to hunker down with guests and enjoy the comforts of home while gathering around a dish of something warm and delicious.

WEEKNIGHT SUPPERS

Meatloaf with Crispy Onions

Grown-Up Grilled Cheese

Pork Pot Stickers

Sloppy Joes

Poblano Mushroom Quesadillas

Fried Chicken Sammies with Slaw

Everything Slaw

WEEKEND SUPPERS

Chicken Tikka Masala

Veggie Tortilla Soup

Posole Southern Style

Pearl Onion and Mushroom Risotto

HOT LITTLE EXTRAS

Naan

Roasted Poblano Queso with Avocado Salsa

Fried Squash with Pimento Cheese

Indian-Spiced Roasted Okra and Tomatoes

Roasted Tomato and Zucchini Tart

Cornbread Dressing

DRINKS AND DESSERTS

Tropical Storm

Amaretto Sour

Coffee Crème Brûlée

Triple Treat Brownies

WEEKNIGHT
SUPPERS

MEATLOAF WITH CRISPY ONIONS

Meatloaf is Sarah's favorite. One day, after John took her to a restaurant, she came home raving about the amazing meatloaf she'd eaten. "It had French fries on it!" she said. I've never loved meatloaf, but at the mention of French fries, my interest was piqued. She and I experimented in the kitchen, but despite many tries, it never came out quite right. My mother suggested we try making it free form on a sheet pan rather than in a loaf pan to get a crispier texture. That made a huge improvement. But the French fry topping still wasn't working. Finally, I fried up some onion rings instead. As Sarah excitedly sat down to eat, she said, "Oh yeah. It wasn't French fries. It was onion rings." Well, now we know! And it is amazing.

Makes 4 to 6 servings

MEATLOAF

Nonstick cooking spray

1 pound ground beef

1 pound ground pork

2 large eggs

1/2 cup grated Parmesan
    cheese

1 cup fresh bread crumbs

(about 2 to 3 slices of
    bread, crusts removed)

4 cloves garlic, minced
    (about 4 teaspoons)

1/4 white onion, minced
    (about 1/4 cup)

2 teaspoons dried thyme

Salt and freshly ground
    coarse black
    pepper to taste

3/4 cup ketchup, divided

FRIED ONIONS

1 large Vidalia onion,
    thinly sliced (or other
    sweet yellow onion)

1/2 cup buttermilk

1 cup canola oil

1 cup all-purpose flour

1/2 teaspoon cayenne
    pepper

1 teaspoon salt plus more
    for sprinkling

1/2 teaspoon freshly ground
    coarse black pepper

1. Preheat the oven to 350 degrees.
2. Line a rimmed baking sheet with foil. Place a wire rack on top and cover it with foil. Using a knife, slit a few holes in the foil, so the meatloaf grease can drain down onto the baking sheet. Spray the foil lightly with the cooking spray.
3. In a large bowl, gently combine the ground beef, pork, eggs, Parmesan, bread crumbs, garlic, minced onions, thyme, salt and pepper, and 1/2 cup of the ketchup.
4. Shape the meat into a loaf (about 9 inches long) on the foil-covered wire rack on top of the baking sheet.
5. Top the loaf with the remaining 1/4 cup of ketchup and bake for 45 to 60 minutes, or until the internal temperature reaches 160 degrees. Remove the

meatloaf from the oven and let it rest for 10 minutes before slicing.

6. While the meatloaf is baking, make the fried onions. In a medium bowl, combine the onions and buttermilk. Let them sit for 20 minutes.

7. While the onions are soaking, in a cast-iron skillet, heat the oil to 350 degrees.

8. In a shallow dish, combine the flour, cayenne, salt, and pepper.

9. Using tongs, shake the excess buttermilk off the onion slices and dip them into the flour mixture, tossing to coat. Shake the excess flour off the onions and, working in batches, being sure not to overcrowd the pan, carefully place them in the hot oil. Fry the onions until they are golden brown and crisp, flipping once. Remove the onions from the skillet and let them drain on paper towels. Sprinkle the onions with salt.

10. Slice the meatloaf and top each slice with a handful of fried onions to serve.

GROWN-UP GRILLED CHEESE

We travel a lot for volleyball, and sometimes that means staying in cookie-cutter hotels and eating cookie-cutter food. But one time we were lucky enough to stay at the Graduate Columbia hotel in South Carolina. Sarah and I arrived late and hungry, so we bellied up to the hotel bar, and she ordered a grilled cheese and tomato soup. As I ate my own food, I couldn't stop staring at Sarah's grilled cheese. She gave me a few bites, and I was hooked. As soon as we got home, I said, "Let's make that grilled cheese!" Now this elevated grilled cheese is a Morey family fave we enjoy at least once a week.

Makes 1 sandwich ♡

3 tablespoons mayonnaise	2 slices thick, country-style white bread	I cup shredded Cheddar cheese (4-ounce block)
2 tablespoons pesto	I tablespoon butter	

1. In a small bowl, combine the mayonnaise and pesto.
2. Spread I tablespoon of the mixture on one side of each piece of bread.
3. Heat a cast-iron skillet over medium heat and add the butter.
4. Place one piece of bread, pesto side down, in the skillet. Add the cheese and top with the remaining piece of bread, pesto side up.
5. Cook for 3 to 4 minutes on each side, or until the cheese has melted and the bread is crisp.
6. Remove the sandwich from the skillet, cut in half, and serve.

PORK POT STICKERS

My girls beg me for these pot stickers. They taste delicious and are fun to make. You can prepare a bunch at a time and then freeze them to use whenever you need a quick meal. Here are the two keys to using the wonton wrappers: avoid loading them up with too much meat and have the bowl of water handy so you can dip your fingers and seal the wonton wrappers without them drying out.

Makes 8 to 10 servings (52 pot stickers)

- 2 tablespoons toasted sesame oil
- 2 cups thinly sliced napa cabbage (about 7 ounces)
- 2 tablespoons minced garlic (about 8 cloves), divided

- 1 tablespoon minced fresh ginger plus 1 tablespoon grated fresh ginger, divided
- 7 tablespoons minced green onions, divided (7 to 8 green onions depending on size)

- 1 pound ground pork
- 1 tablespoon soy sauce
- 52 wonton wrappers
- Water
- 1 tablespoon vegetable oil

DIPPING SAUCE

- 3 tablespoons soy sauce
- 1 tablespoon fish sauce
- 2 tablespoons water
- 1 tablespoon lime juice

- 1 tablespoon rice wine vinegar
- 2 teaspoons brown or palm sugar

- 2 teaspoons minced fresh ginger
- 1 green onion, sliced

1. To make the dipping sauce: In a small bowl, combine the soy sauce, fish sauce, water, lime juice, vinegar, brown sugar, ginger, and green onion.

2. In a large skillet, heat the sesame oil over medium heat. Add the cabbage, 1 tablespoon of the garlic, the tablespoon of minced ginger, and 3 tablespoons of the green onions. Sauté until the cabbage is tender, about 6 to 8 minutes, stirring frequently. Remove the skillet from the heat and let it cool.

3. While the cabbage is cooling, in a medium bowl, combine the pork, soy sauce, grated ginger, the remaining tablespoon of garlic, and 3 tablespoons of the green onions. Add the pork mixture to the cooled cabbage and mix well to combine.

4. Fill a small bowl with water and have ready a rimmed baking sheet and a damp paper towel. Place 1 tablespoon of the pork mixture in the center of a wonton wrapper. Dip your finger in the water and run it around the edge of the wrapper. Fold the wrapper over in half to create a triangle shape, pinching the edges to seal it well. Place the filled pot stickers on the baking sheet and cover

POBLANO MUSHROOM QUESADILLAS

Like pretty much every other kid in America, my children would eat quesadillas every night for supper if I let them. This is my quesadilla compromise: the flavors I want to eat in the crispy, cheesy triangles they love. A meatless meal the whole family can get excited about!

Makes 4 servings

3 poblano peppers

2 tablespoons butter

1 pound mushrooms, sliced

½ teaspoon cumin

½ teaspoon coriander

1 teaspoon chili powder

Salt to taste

½ cup beer, water, or
    chicken stock

1 bunch fresh cilantro,
    tied into a bundle
    with kitchen twine

2 tablespoons bacon
    grease, butter, or
    vegetable oil

8 flour or corn tortillas
    (5 to 6 inches
    in diameter)

16 ounces shredded
    Monterey Jack
    cheese, divided

Pico de gallo for garnish

Chopped avocado
    for garnish

1. To roast the poblanos: Using tongs, hold the peppers right over the open flame of a gas stove burner. Turn them as they get black. If you don't have a gas stove, put the peppers on a rimmed baking sheet and broil them in the oven. Once they cool, remove the bubbled (blistered) skin. Cut the peppers open, remove the seeds, and chop.

2. In a sauté pan over medium heat, add the butter. Add the mushrooms and cook for 5 minutes, stirring occasionally.

3. Add the cumin, coriander, chili powder, and salt. Stir to coat the mushrooms. Add the beer or liquid of your choice and stir. Add the cilantro bundle and cover the pan. Cook for 20 minutes, or until all of the liquid has absorbed.

4. Remove the mushrooms from the pan and set aside. Wipe out the pan, add the bacon grease or fat of your choice, and heat over medium heat.

5. Add one tortilla to the pan. Top it with ½ cup (or more if you want!) of the cheese, ¼ cup of the mushrooms, and 1 tablespoon of the chopped poblanos. Place another tortilla on top and press down with a spatula. Cook for 2 to 3 minutes on each side, or until the tortillas are crisp and golden and the cheese has melted.

6. Let the quesadillas cool for 2 minutes before cutting, then garnish with the pico de gallo and avocado to serve.

FRIED CHICKEN SAMMIES WITH SLAW

Our kitchen is so small at our Charleston Callie's Hot Little Biscuit that we've never been able to make our own fried chicken. There's no room for a commercial fryer and vent system. So I was very excited when we opened in Charlotte and could have a fryer. But I was a little intimidated too. It's not easy to make great fried chicken consistently on a large scale. The first step was to create the perfect blend of flavors. Then perfecting the dry-wet-dry dipping process for that extra-crispy crunch. Like my Jerk Chicken recipe, the hardest part of this one is assembling the huge list of spices, but it's well worth it! It doesn't even need salt because there is already a ton of flavor. The spices and the texture come together beautifully, especially paired in the end with a buttery bun, Sriracha mayo, pickles, and slaw.

Makes 6 servings

3 cups buttermilk

½ cup pickle juice

6 boneless, skinless
 chicken breasts

3 cups self-rising flour

2 tablespoons freshly
 ground coarse
 black pepper

2 tablespoons paprika

1 tablespoon onion powder

1 tablespoon dried oregano

1 tablespoon garlic salt

2 teaspoons dry mustard

1 teaspoon dried thyme

1 teaspoon dried basil

1 teaspoon celery seed

½ teaspoon cayenne
 pepper

1 cup canola oil

½ cup mayonnaise

2 teaspoons Sriracha

6 brioche buns, buttered
 and toasted

Pickles for topping

Everything Slaw for
 topping (page 155)

1. In a large bowl, combine the buttermilk and pickle juice. Add the chicken and marinate it in the mixture for 1 hour.

2. In another large bowl, combine the flour, pepper, paprika, onion powder, oregano, garlic salt, dry mustard, thyme, basil, celery seed, and cayenne.

3. In a large cast-iron skillet, heat the oil to 350 degrees.

4. While the oil is heating, prepare the chicken. Shake the excess buttermilk off each chicken breast and roll it lightly in the seasoned flour. Dip the breast in the buttermilk mixture again, gently shaking off the excess buttermilk. Roll again in the seasoned flour, making

sure to heavily coat the chicken. Place the coated chicken breasts on a wire rack until you're ready to fry.

5. Carefully place the chicken in the skillet with the hot oil, frying only 3 breasts at a time. Fry for 6 to 8 minutes on each side, or until the internal temperature is 165 degrees. If the chicken gets too brown and isn't cooked fully, place it on a wire rack in a 250-degree oven until the chicken reaches 165 degrees. Make sure the oil doesn't go over 350 to 360 degrees. Constantly watch the oil temperature. If it gets too low, you can put a lid over it to bring it up to temperature quickly.

6. In a small bowl, combine the mayonnaise and Sriracha and stir.

7. Serve the chicken on toasted brioche buns with the Sriracha mayonnaise and topped with pickles and Everything Slaw.

HOT LITTLE TIP

Make and Take a Bucket of Chicken

Use the same ingredients and process to fry bone-in, skin-on wings, thighs, legs, and breasts. You can also fry boneless, skinless thighs—or slice boneless breasts before frying and make chicken strips. A bucket of homemade fried chicken is perfect for a weekend tailgate! Keep the fried chicken warm on a wire rack on a rimmed baking sheet in a 200-degree oven until just before you're ready to go. Then pack the chicken up right before you leave the house.

Here's another one of my favorite ways to serve fried chicken on the go: I line a brown paper grocery bag with parchment paper, add the chicken, and roll the bag shut. Then when I'm ready to serve, I tear open the paper bag and serve with a bottle of hot sauce on the spread-out paper for a rustic presentation.

EVERYTHING SLAW

This is a crunchy salad I love to serve with grilled chicken or fish, on burgers, hot dogs, fried fish sammies, and of course, fried chicken sammies. Basically . . . everything.

Makes 7 1/2 cups

1/2 head purple or green cabbage (or a mixture of both), very thinly sliced (about 4 cups)

1/2 cup chopped fresh flat-leaf Italian parsley

1/2 cup chopped fresh cilantro

1/2 jalapeño pepper, very thinly sliced

4 radishes, very thinly sliced into matchsticks

1/4 cup diced red onion

1 seedless cucumber, quartered and chopped

1 red bell pepper, chopped (about 1 cup)

DRESSING

1 1/2 tablespoons Dijon mustard

1/2 tablespoon minced shallot

Zest of 1/2 lemon (about 1 teaspoon)

1/4 cup red wine vinegar

3/4 cup olive oil

Salt and freshly ground coarse black pepper to taste

1. To make the dressing: In a small bowl, combine the Dijon mustard, shallot, lemon zest, vinegar, olive oil, and salt and pepper and whisk together.

2. In a large bowl, combine the cabbage, parsley, cilantro, jalapeño, radishes, onions, cucumber, and bell peppers and toss.

3. Add the dressing to the cabbage mixture a little at a time and toss to combine. (You may not need to use all of the dressing—start with 1/2 cup and adjust.) Serve immediately or cover with plastic wrap and refrigerate until ready to serve.

HOT LITTLE TIP

Hot Little Shallot

I love to put half a shallot in a foil pouch drizzled with olive oil and salt and pepper and roast it for 30 minutes in a 350-degree oven before mincing. Makes this dressing even more yummy . . . and makes your kitchen smell amazing!

Note: You can add more veggies to this slaw recipe if you want to bulk it up for a side dish instead of a sandwich topper.

HOT LITTLE TIPS

Tailgating Trade Secrets

Whether it's a football game or the rodeo, I love to tailgate. Taking a party along with me is one of my favorite ways to entertain. Over the years, I have developed a few tricks of the trade that make it easier and more fun. It's all about convenience. The better job you do packing it in, the easier it is to pack it all up when it's time to go home.

- If you have a pickup truck or SUV with a tailgate or an SUV with a rear door, skip bringing a bulky table along. Instead, pack a tablecloth, spread it over the truck bed or rear space, then use height to display items at different levels. You can even do this out of the trunk of a car. To create platforms, turn plastic storage containers upside down, drape cardboard boxes with a tablecloth, or use cake stands and platters.
- To display napkins or silverware, use interesting old cans, cups, or mason jars. I like to serve breadsticks from a jar on a crudités platter.
- Use cute paper plates and napkins that can be thrown away.
- Pack reusable, not disposable, plastic cups for drinks.
- For the drinks cooler, pack separate resealable plastic bags with ice for drinks. That way, the ice that goes in the cups stays clean and separate from the ice in the cooler with the cans and bottles.
- When packing a cooler, remember that heat rises, so put the ice on top, not the bottom. The cold packs from Callie's Hot Little Biscuit shipments are a great less-wet alternative to ice that you can put on top of food in a cooler and use over and over again.
- Extra-pro tip from my friend Nathalie Dupree: pack an extra cooler. One or two for storing ice, drinks, and food and one with water and dish soap in it. When it's time to pack up, toss the used cups and dirty serving pieces into the cooler and let them soak the whole way home for easy clean-up later. Thank you, Nathalie!
- Pack a trash bag for trash and pack a grocery bag for the tablecloth and any other linens you bring. When you unload the car at home, take the linens bag straight to the laundry room.
- For sandwiches, pack every part separately and wait to assemble them when you arrive at your tailgating spot, so the bread doesn't get soggy. If you're making tomato sandwiches, for example, slice the tomatoes ahead of time and put them in their own plastic container. Pack the bread, mayo, and knife for spreading, and salt and pepper. Make the sandwiches when you get there and display to serve. For Fried Chicken Sammies, pack the chicken in a paper bag to keep it crispy. If you're more worried about keeping it moist and warm, pack it in foil. Pack the buns, Sriracha mayo, pickles, and slaw in separate containers to assemble the sammies on-site.

- For traveling cocktails, make drinks in bulk ahead of time and pack them in quart containers in a cooler.
- If the weather is warm, double up on serving bowls and put ice in one and set the other on top to keep the contents cool. Keep half of cold dips in the cooler and then replenish what's on display with the fresh dip as needed. If you're worried about bugs, bring your cutest kitchen towels to drape over the food or invest in a set of food tents.

TRAVEL-WELL TREATS

These treats can be made ahead and withstand a long day in and out of the cooler. (Recipes marked with an asterisk [*] are taken from my first cookbook, *Callie's Biscuits and Southern Traditions*.)

Crowd Pleasers

- Fried Chicken Sammies (page 153; or a bucket of homemade fried chicken)
- Pickled Shrimp*
- Frito Pie*
- Lemon-Thyme Chicken Wings*

Small Bites

- Buttermilk Biscuits with county ham or sausage (page 5)
- Mom's Perfect Tomato Sandwiches*
- Boiled Peanuts
- Fiery Cheese Wafers*
- Fiery Pimento Cheese–Laced "Naughty" Eggs*

Dips

- French Feta Dip (page 70)
- Butter Bean Hummus (page 122)
- Serve both with veggies and artisanal crackers

Desserts

- Killer Cookies (page 133)
- Triple Treat Brownies (page 189)
- Oatmeal Cream Pies*

Drinks

- Tropical Storms (page 183)
- Morey Margaritas*

WEEKEND
SUPPERS

CHICKEN TIKKA MASALA

I love Indian food. When I lived in New York, I ate it three or four times a week. After John and I started dating, he told me he loved it too. That made me happy, and we had many spicy meals together. About a year after we got married, the truth came out: he did not love Indian food. I was touched by his sweet white lie during our courtship, but I was also determined to change his mind. With this dish, I did!

Makes 4 to 6 servings   (W)

2 pounds boneless, skinless chicken thighs

1 tablespoon ground coriander

1 1/2 teaspoons cumin

1 1/2 teaspoons paprika

1 1/2 teaspoons turmeric

1/2 teaspoon ground cardamom

1/2 teaspoon ground nutmeg

3/4 teaspoon garam masala

1/2 teaspoon cayenne pepper

1/2 cup plain whole-milk Greek yogurt

2 tablespoons olive oil

2 teaspoons fresh lime or lemon juice

8 cloves garlic, minced, divided

4 tablespoons butter

1 large white onion, finely chopped (about 1 cup)

2 tablespoons grated fresh ginger

1 (28-ounce) can tomato puree

3/4 cup water

1 1/4 teaspoons salt

1/2 teaspoon freshly ground coarse black pepper

Nonstick cooking spray

1/2 cup heavy whipping cream or half-and-half

1/2 cup chopped fresh cilantro plus more for garnish

Cooked rice for serving

Cumin seeds, optional for extra spice

Lime wedges for garnish

1. Cut the chicken thighs into 1 1/2-inch pieces.

2. In a small bowl, combine the coriander, cumin, paprika, turmeric, cardamom, nutmeg, garam masala, and cayenne.

3. In a medium bowl, combine the chicken, yogurt, olive oil, lime or lemon juice, and half of the minced garlic. Add half of the spice mixture and toss to coat the chicken. Let the chicken marinate for 60 minutes.

4. While the chicken is marinating, make the sauce. In a large sauté pan or Dutch oven, melt the butter over medium heat. Add the onions and cook until the onions are soft and translucent.

5. Add the ginger and the remaining garlic and cook for 2 to 3 minutes. Add the remaining half of the spice mixture and stir to combine. Add the tomato puree, water, salt, and pepper. Let the sauce simmer for 30 minutes, stirring occasionally.

6. Turn the oven broiler to high heat. Line a rimmed baking sheet with foil and place a wire rack on top. Spray the rack with nonstick cooking spray. Place the chicken pieces on the rack. Broil for 8 to 10 minutes, turning once, until

the chicken begins to get some char. Remove the pan from the oven. The chicken will not be fully cooked—it will continue to cook in the sauce.

7. Add the chicken and pan drippings to the sauce and let it simmer for another 15 minutes, stirring occasionally.

8. After 15 minutes, turn off the heat and add the heavy cream and chopped cilantro. Stir until combined.

9. Add the cumin seeds to the rice, if using.

10. Serve the sauce over the cooked rice. Garnish with fresh cilantro and a squeeze of the lime wedges.

Note: I like to serve this with my Indian-Spiced Roasted Okra and Tomatoes (page 175), Naan (page 171), and raita.

HOT LITTLE TIP

Store Some Spice & Save Some Time

Mixing all the spices together is the hardest part of making tikka masala! As I measure out the spices into the bowl, I also measure them into a plastic container and then label the container with masking tape. That way, the spices are already measured, mixed, and ready to go next time.

VEGGIE TORTILLA SOUP

I came up with this recipe for our company retreat. There were fifty people there, and it was the first time the whole company was filmed for *How She Rolls*. I wanted to create something warm and flavorful that worked with everyone's dietary restrictions and preferences that was also bright and fun to eat to celebrate the occasion. The soup was a huge hit! Everyone could customize it in taste and texture with a wide range of accoutrements. I even brought along some Schug (page 221), a super-spicy green hot sauce. The secret to the depth of flavor for this soup is sautéing the vegetables in the oil used to fry the tortillas. This one is a comfort food crowd pleaser, perfect for a chilly afternoon with the whole crew.

Makes 8 to 10 servings

- 2 poblano peppers
- 4 tablespoons canola or vegetable oil
- 8 corn tortillas, cut into strips about ¼ inch wide
- Salt to taste
- 1 red bell pepper, diced (about 1 cup)
- 1 onion, diced (about 1 cup)
- 6 cloves garlic, minced (about 6 teaspoons)

- 1 tablespoon cumin
- 1 teaspoon coriander
- 1 teaspoon chipotle chili powder (or more for more heat)
- Zest and juice of 2 limes, divided (about 2 teaspoons zest and 3 to 4 tablespoons juice)
- 2 (28-ounce) cans fire-roasted tomatoes
- 8 cups vegetable broth

- 1 bunch fresh cilantro, tied into a bundle with kitchen twine

> ### HOT LITTLE TIP
>
> Poblanos can be sneaky. Most are mild, but some can fire up a dish with spice. Beware!

Accoutrements

- Diced tomatoes
- Lime wedges
- Thinly sliced radishes
- Sliced jalapeño peppers

- Broiled corn
- Cilantro
- Cotija cheese
- Chorizo

- Shredded chicken
- Schug (page 221)

1. To roast the poblanos: Using tongs, hold the peppers right over the open flame of a gas stove burner. Turn them as they get black. If you don't have a gas stove, put the peppers on a rimmed baking sheet and broil them in the oven. Once they cool, remove the bubbled (blistered) skin. Cut the peppers open, remove the seeds, and chop.

2. In a Dutch oven, heat the oil over medium-high heat. Once the oil reaches 350 degrees, carefully add the tortilla strips, working in batches, making sure not to overcrowd the pot. Fry the strips

until they are crisp and golden brown. Remove the strips from the pot and place them on a paper towel–lined plate. Immediately sprinkle them with salt.

3. After frying the strips, drain half of the oil from the Dutch oven. Add the chopped poblanos, bell peppers, onions, and garlic. Sauté until the vegetables are tender, about 6 to 7 minutes.

4. Add half of the tortilla strips to the vegetables. Set aside the other half of the strips to serve with the accoutrements.

5. Add the cumin, coriander, chili powder, and lime zest. Stir to combine. Add the fire-roasted tomatoes.

6. Using an immersion blender, carefully blend the soup until it's smooth. (Or place the soup in a blender, blend until smooth, and return the soup to the pot—but be careful because the soup will be very hot.)

7. Add the vegetable broth and lime juice. Stir to combine.

8. Add the cilantro bundle to the soup. Bring the soup to a boil, then reduce the heat to low. Let it simmer for 30 minutes. Serve the soup with the tortilla strips and other accoutrements for topping.

Note: I recommend Kitchen Basics brand vegetable stock.

POSOLE SOUTHERN STYLE

Posole is a soup traditionally served with hominy. My grandmother called grits "hominy," so I always thought grits and hominy were the same thing. But hominy is the whole kernel of corn with the hull removed. Grits is coarsely ground corn, often ground hominy. As I love to do in my culinary adventures, I wanted to combine the traditional flavors with my own Southern traditions, so I switched out the hominy for grits. If you're not a grits fan, you could serve this over rice instead, but the creamy golden grits at the bottom of the bowl make the perfect ending to this tasty soup.

Makes 8 to 10 servings   〇 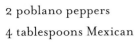 ⓦ

2 poblano peppers

4 tablespoons Mexican dry rub

1 (4-pound) bone-in pork butt

2 tablespoons bacon grease (or olive oil, vegetable oil, or canola oil), divided

½ white onion, diced (about ½ cup)

3 cloves garlic, minced (about 3 teaspoons)

2 bell peppers, diced (green, red, orange, or yellow—whichever you prefer, about 2 cups)

64 ounces chicken stock

Salt and freshly ground

coarse black pepper to taste

Cooked grits for serving

Chopped avocado for garnish

Cotija (or feta) cheese, crumbled, for garnish

Lime wedges for garnish

Chopped cilantro for garnish

MEXICAN DRY RUB

2 teaspoons paprika

2 tablespoons chili powder

2 teaspoons cumin

1 tablespoon onion powder

2 teaspoons garlic powder

2 teaspoons dried oregano

½ teaspoon cayenne pepper

1 teaspoon sugar

1 teaspoon salt

1. To roast the poblanos: Using tongs, hold the peppers right over the open flame of a gas stove burner. Turn them as they get black. If you don't have a gas stove, put the peppers on a rimmed baking sheet and broil them in the oven. Once they cool, remove the bubbled (blistered) skin. Cut the peppers open, remove the seeds, and chop.

2. Preheat the oven to 275 degrees.

3. To make the dry rub: In a small bowl, combine the paprika, chili powder, cumin, onion powder, garlic powder, oregano, cayenne, sugar, and salt.

4. Rub the pork butt all over with 4 tablespoons of the dry rub and set aside.

5. In a 5-quart Dutch oven, heat 1 tablespoon of the bacon grease over medium heat. Add the onions, garlic, poblanos, and bell peppers. Sauté until the vegetables are soft, about 8 to 10 minutes, stirring occasionally.

6. Remove the vegetables from the pot and add the remaining tablespoon of bacon grease. Increase the heat to medium high.

7. Add the pork and sear for 2 minutes on all sides. Add the vegetables back to the pot with the pork. Add the chicken stock. If needed, add up to 2 cups of water. Season with salt and pepper. Cover and cook in the oven for 3 hours. Taste and adjust to your taste with more of the Mexican Dry Rub and salt and pepper.

8. Remove the bone and fatty pieces from the meat. Using two forks, shred the meat in the pot. Let the meat cool to room temperature, then place the pot in the refrigerator overnight.

9. The next day, remove the pot from the refrigerator and scrape off the layer of fat from the top.

10. Reheat the pot over medium heat. Once warm, serve the meat over creamy grits, garnished with the avocado, Cotija cheese, lime wedges, and cilantro.

PEARL ONION AND MUSHROOM RISOTTO

This dish is luscious. It feels like a splurge, like a restaurant meal at home. I love to serve this to people, including children, who say they don't like mushrooms—it changes their mind every time! You can serve this as a vegetarian meal or as a side for seared steak, pork roast, or shrimp. It does require some attention, and you need to be ready to sit down and eat as soon as it comes together. I like to have the table set and a large serving bowl or platter on hand and ready. I invite the party into the kitchen for cocktails, so we can socialize while I stir, and then we all move to the table as soon as the risotto is ready. A true dinner party stunner.

Makes 4 to 6 servings

- 1 tablespoon olive oil
- 7 tablespoons butter, divided
- ½ (12-ounce) bag frozen pearl onions
- 10 sprigs fresh thyme
- 1 cup dry white wine, divided
- 1 (8-ounce) container

- cremini mushrooms, sliced
- 8 cups chicken stock
- 1 small white onion, finely chopped (about ½ cup)
- 3 cloves garlic, minced (about 3 teaspoons)
- 2 cups raw Arborio

- rice, rinsed a few times and drained
- 1 cup grated Parmesan cheese plus extra for garnish
- Salt to taste
- Chopped fresh flat-leaf Italian parsley for garnish

1. Preheat the oven to 200 degrees.

2. In a sauté pan, heat the olive oil and 2 tablespoons of the butter over medium heat.

3. Add the pearl onions and sauté until they begin to brown, about 8 to 10 minutes. Add the thyme and ½ cup of the wine. Cover with a lid, reduce the heat to medium low, and cook for 30 minutes, stirring occasionally.

4. While the pearl onions are cooking, heat another sauté pan over medium heat. Add the mushrooms and 2 tablespoons of the butter. Cover with a lid, reduce the heat to medium low, and cook for 20 to 30 minutes, stirring occasionally.

5. Once the pearl onions and mushrooms have cooked, combine them into one pan. Place the pan in the oven to keep them warm while you cook the risotto.

6. In a large saucepan, bring the chicken stock to a simmer.

7. While the chicken stock is simmering, heat a Dutch oven or large pot over medium heat. Add the remaining 3 tablespoons of the butter. Once the butter has melted, add the white onions and garlic. Cook until the onions are tender, about 5 to 7 minutes. Add the rice and stir to combine. Add the remaining ½ cup of white wine and cook until the wine has absorbed, stirring frequently, about 3 to 5 minutes.

8. Once the wine has absorbed, begin

adding the warm chicken stock 2 to 3 ladles at a time, stirring constantly. The rice may not absorb all the stock. Taste for tenderness after 30 to 40 minutes of cooking. The rice should become creamy in appearance, and if you crush a kernel, the exterior will be softened with a faint bit of white in the middle.

9. Turn off the heat and add the Parmesan, stirring to combine. Add salt if needed.

10. Transfer the risotto to a serving bowl and top with the pearl onions and mushrooms. Garnish with the extra Parmesan and parsley and serve.

HOT

LITTLE

EXTRAS

NAAN

I started researching how to make naan bread when I found myself buying it all the time! When I discovered you could make it using self-rising flour, I got even more interested because I always have my White Lily self-rising on hand for biscuits. I added some red onion and garlic and was instantly hooked on the result. Homemade naan is way too simple and delicious to ever settle for store-bought again.

Makes 8 rounds

2 cups self-rising flour,
   1/3 cup reserved
   for dusting
1 teaspoon salt
3/4 to 1 cup plain yogurt

1/2 cup diced red onion
3 cloves minced garlic
   (about 3 teaspoons)
Vegetable oil for frying

2 tablespoons butter,
   melted
1/3 cup chopped cilantro
   for garnish

1. In a large bowl, combine 1 2/3 cups of the flour and the salt.

2. The amount of yogurt to add will depend on the brand of yogurt because some are thicker than others. Add 3/4 cup of the yogurt to the flour and salt to start, then add more by the tablespoon until you create a soft dough.

3. Add the onions and garlic. On a lightly floured piece of parchment paper, knead the dough until it's smooth. Place the dough in a bowl, cover with plastic wrap, and allow it to rest for 30 minutes.

4. Roll the dough into an 8-inch-long log. Cut the log into 8 pieces and gently shape each into a ball.

5. Heat a cast-iron skillet over medium heat and brush with vegetable oil. Preheat the oven to 200 degrees.

6. Roll out the dough balls into 6-inch circles and brush with vegetable oil. Cook each naan 2 minutes per side in the oiled skillet.

7. As each one finishes cooking in the skillet, place it on a rack in the oven to stay warm until all of the naan are cooked.

8. Generously brush the top of each naan with the melted butter.

9. Top with the cilantro and serve while hot.

Note: I prefer White Lily Unbleached Self-Rising Flour.

ROASTED POBLANO QUESO WITH AVOCADO SALSA

Like most people, I am a sucker for melted white cheese. It's easy to re-create the restaurant version at home, but it did take some testing and experimenting to get it just right. The secret is a bit of American cheese. The salsa is a refreshing, healthy, and visually pleasing complement. Add a margarita, and this queso and salsa combo is a meal in itself.

Makes 4 to 6 servings

1 poblano pepper

1 cup half-and-half

1 teaspoon cornstarch

4 ounces shredded Monterey Jack cheese

4 ounces shredded extra-sharp white Cheddar

4 ounces sliced white American cheese

1 teaspoon cumin

1 teaspoon coriander

1/2 teaspoon cayenne pepper

4 thin slices jalapeño pepper

Tostadas or chips to serve

1. To roast the poblano: Using tongs, hold the pepper right over the open flame of a gas stove burner. Turn it as it gets black. If you don't have a gas stove, put the pepper on a rimmed baking sheet and broil it in the oven. Once it cools, remove the bubbled (blistered) skin. Cut the pepper open, remove the seeds, and chop.

2. In a saucepan over medium-low heat, combine the half-and-half and cornstarch and whisk for 1 minute. Add the Monterey Jack, Cheddar, and American cheeses, cumin, coriander, and cayenne. Whisk until the cheeses have melted. Keep the heat low to keep the cheese from turning grainy.

3. Reduce the heat to low. Add the chopped poblano and jalapeño slices. Stir for 1 minute, or until the queso is smooth. Remove the pan from the heat and serve hot with tostadas and/or chips.

AVOCADO SALSA

3 fresh tomatoes, peeled and chopped

1 bunch fresh cilantro, chopped (about 1 cup)

1/2 red onion, chopped (about 1/3 cup)

Juice of 1/2 lime (about 1 tablespoon juice)

1/2 jalapeño pepper, seeds removed and minced

3 tablespoons olive oil

Salt and freshly ground coarse black pepper to taste

2 avocados, diced

In a medium bowl, combine the tomatoes, cilantro, onions, lime juice, jalapeño, olive oil, and salt and pepper. Chill for 3 minutes. Just before serving, gently fold in the avocados.

FRIED SQUASH WITH PIMENTO CHEESE

When I was little, my dad would take me to Miss Kitty's, a meat-and-three in Charleston, where fried squash was one of their incredible Southern sides. To this day, fried squash reminds me of sitting at the counter with my dad while he chatted with Miss Kitty. I barely liked squash, but when fried, it was like a completely different food! I witnessed a similar awe when I led a cooking class for a group of women from up North. The class included lunch, and I made this dish. You would have thought I served those ladies the rarest, most cherished delicacy on the planet.

Makes 10 to 12 servings (about 30 to 35 squash rounds)

1 cup canola oil

1 cup pimento cheese

1 cup all-purpose flour

2 teaspoons salt plus more for sprinkling

1 teaspoon freshly ground coarse black pepper

2 large eggs, lightly beaten

2 yellow squash, sliced into ¼-inch rounds

¼ cup chopped chives for garnish

> ## HOT LITTLE TIP
>
> ### Squash Sammies
>
> Using a melon baller, top a squash slice with pimento cheese, then cover it with a second slice. Press gently, then roll the sammies in chopped chives or even nuts. A fun appetizer or nutritious snack!

1. In a cast-iron skillet or other heavy-duty pot, heat the oil over medium-high heat until it reaches 350 degrees.

2. Place the pimento cheese in a quart-size resealable plastic bag. Cut a small corner off the bag to make a piping bag. Leave it out and let it warm to room temperature.

3. In a shallow dish, combine the flour, salt, and pepper. Place the eggs in another shallow dish.

4. Dip each squash round into the flour, then into the eggs, and then back to the flour, coating the squash thoroughly. Place the battered squash on a wire rack.

5. Add 6 squash rounds at a time to the hot oil, being careful not to splash the oil. It's important not to overcrowd the pan, as that will lower the temperature of the oil and the squash won't get as crispy. Fry the squash on each side until they turn golden brown, 1 to 2 minutes.

6. With a wire or metal skimmer or tongs, carefully remove the squash and place them on a clean wire rack or a plate lined with paper towels and immediately sprinkle them with salt.

7. Once the fried squash rounds have cooled just a little bit, pipe about a teaspoon of pimento cheese onto each round. Sprinkle with chives and serve immediately.

Note: I prefer my Callie's Fiery Pimento Cheese.

INDIAN-SPICED ROASTED OKRA AND TOMATOES

This recipe is a play on the Southern tradition of stewed okra and tomatoes. It's a quick and easy way to create the flavors that normally take hours on the stove to develop, and it's enhanced by some of my favorite Indian spices. Another example of the cross-cultural culinary connections I love to celebrate.

Makes 4 servings

1 pound okra, tops cut off and cut in half lengthwise

1 pint heirloom cherry tomatoes, cut into halves

1/4 teaspoon cumin

1/4 teaspoon coriander

1/8 teaspoon turmeric

3 tablespoons olive oil

Salt and freshly ground coarse black pepper to taste

1. Preheat the oven to 425 degrees. Line a rimmed baking sheet with parchment paper.
2. In a large bowl, combine the okra, tomatoes, cumin, coriander, turmeric, olive oil, and salt and pepper and toss.
3. Pour the mixture onto the baking sheet.
4. Bake for 20 to 30 minutes, or until the vegetables are slightly charred, and serve.

Note: You can serve this as a side or over rice as a vegetarian main dish.

ROASTED TOMATO AND ZUCCHINI TART

The smell of these vegetables roasting in the oven will make you a fan of this tart before you even taste it! I discovered my love of roasted tomatoes when we were trying to come up with some vegetarian options for biscuit toppings at Callie's Hot Little Biscuit. The roasted tomatoes were a surprise favorite and have become a super-popular item. You can make a meal of this tart or slice it and serve it as a colorful, savory hors d'oeuvre.

Makes 4 to 6 servings

3 cups thinly sliced zucchini (about 3 zucchinis)

3 cups halved mixed medley of cherry tomatoes

2 cloves garlic, minced (about 2 teaspoons)

2 green onions, diced

2 tablespoons olive oil

Salt and freshly ground coarse black pepper to taste

1 tablespoon all-purpose flour, divided

1 sheet puff pastry, thawed

(a brand made with butter preferred)

3 ounces Boursin cheese

1 tablespoon butter, melted

2 tablespoons chopped shelled pistachios

1 tablespoon chopped fresh mint

1. Preheat the oven to 400 degrees. Line a rimmed baking sheet with parchment paper.

2. In a large bowl, combine the zucchini, tomatoes, garlic, green onions, olive oil, and salt and pepper. Pour onto the baking sheet.

3. Roast the vegetables in the oven for 10 to 15 minutes.

4. Transfer the vegetables from the baking sheet into a colander to drain off excess liquid. Let the vegetables drain for 10 minutes, shaking off the liquid.

5. Spread a sheet of parchment paper on the counter or work surface. Sprinkle half of the flour onto the parchment paper. Put the puff pastry on the parchment paper. Sprinkle the other half of the flour on top of the pastry so your

rolling pin won't stick. Roll out the puff pastry into a 10 x 12-inch rectangle. Carefully transfer the parchment paper and puff pastry onto a rimmed baking sheet.

6. Layer the zucchini and tomatoes on the puff pastry, leaving a 1- to 2-inch border of pastry all the way around. Pinch off pieces of the Boursin cheese and scatter them around the zucchini and tomatoes.

7. Gently fold up the edges of the pastry all the way around. Brush the edges of the pastry with the melted butter and then sprinkle the edges with freshly ground black pepper.

8. Bake for 30 to 35 minutes, until the tart is golden brown and crisp.

9. Garnish with the pistachios and mint to serve.

CORNBREAD DRESSING

This recipe is an ode to my grandmother Caroline, and along with rice and gravy it's a nonnegotiable must-have for me at Thanksgiving. If someone else is hosting, I am bringing it with me. I mentioned this dressing in my first cookbook but didn't include the recipe—since then, I've had many requests for it. I couldn't write about fall cooking and leave it out! The smell, the texture, the taste, the fact that you can prepare it ahead of time . . . not to mention the ultimate day-after sammie: a pile of cornbread dressing with turkey and spicy cranberry relish slathered in gravy and tucked inside a buttermilk biscuit. My Thanksgiving simply isn't complete without it.

Makes 8 to 10 servings

6 tablespoons butter, divided

3 cups diced onion

2 cups diced celery

Salt and freshly ground

coarse black pepper to taste

7 cups day-old cast-iron buttermilk cornbread, broken into 1-inch cubes (1 recipe of

Cast-Iron Buttermilk Cornbread)

1 tablespoon minced fresh sage

2 cups chicken or vegetable broth

1. In a large cast-iron skillet, heat 1 tablespoon of the butter over medium heat. Add the onions, celery, and salt and pepper. Sauté until the vegetables are slightly softened, about 5 minutes.

2. Transfer the vegetables to a large bowl. Add the cornbread and sage. Mix well to combine.

3. In the same skillet over medium heat, melt 3 tablespoons of the butter. Add the cornbread mixture. Add the broth and stir to moisten the cornbread. Dot the dressing with the remaining 2 tablespoons of butter and season with salt and pepper.

4. Bake until brown and crispy on top, about 40 to 50 minutes.

CAST-IRON BUTTERMILK CORNBREAD

3 slices bacon

1 1/4 cups plus 2 teaspoons cake flour

3/4 cup yellow cornmeal

1/4 cup sugar

2 teaspoons baking powder

1 teaspoon kosher salt

1/2 teaspoon freshly ground coarse black pepper

1 cup buttermilk

1/3 cup heavy whipping cream

1 large egg, beaten

1. Preheat the oven to 400 degrees.

2. In a cast-iron skillet, cook the bacon. Then remove the bacon from the skillet and let it drain on paper towels. Set

aside the skillet with the bacon grease in it. When the bacon has cooled, crumble it.

3. In a large bowl, combine the flour, cornmeal, sugar, baking powder, salt, and pepper and whisk.

4. In a small bowl, combine the buttermilk, heavy cream, and egg. Add it to the dry ingredients and mix well.

5. Heat the skillet with the bacon grease over high heat until very hot but not smoking. Pour the batter into the skillet. Sprinkle the bacon crumbles into the batter or omit the bacon and save it for another purpose.

6. Bake until a toothpick inserted in the center comes out clean, about 15 to 20 minutes. If you're using the cornbread to make Cornbread Dressing, let it cool, cover it, and set it aside for one day before making the dressing.

DRINKS AND DESSERTS

TROPICAL STORM

It's no secret that hurricane season is a busy time in the South. Thankfully, we rarely experience a devastating Category 5 storm like Hugo. Usually, it's a few small hurricanes that turn into tropical storms before they hit. So when John hears "hurricane," instead of thinking *evacuating* or *battening down the hatches*, he's thinking *hurricane party*. Here's one of his crowd-pleasing concoctions to make by the pitcher. No need to wait for a storm!

Makes 20 servings

1 (1-liter) bottle dark rum
1 (1-liter) bottle light rum
1 1/2 cups fresh lime juice
1 cup freshly squeezed
   orange juice

1 cup mango juice
1 cup pineapple juice
1/2 cup passion fruit juice
1/4 cup grenadine
1/2 cup simple syrup

Soda water
Orange slices for garnish

SIMPLE SYRUP

1 cup sugar

1 cup water

1. To make the simple syrup: In a small saucepan over medium heat, combine the sugar and water. Bring the mixture to a low boil. Stir until the sugar dissolves. Turn off the heat, and let it cool completely. Store leftover syrup in a glass jar in the refrigerator for up to 3 weeks.

2. In a large pitcher, combine the dark rum, light rum, lime juice, orange juice, mango juice, pineapple juice, passion fruit juice, grenadine, and simple syrup.

3. Fill a glass with ice. Pour the cocktail so the glass is 3/4 full. Top with soda water.

4. Stir and garnish with an orange slice.

AMARETTO SOUR

The first time I had an amaretto sour, I was on my high school senior cruise. Once the ship left the dock, the legal drinking age was eighteen. That's not to say we knew what we were doing when, after we got dressed up for the first night on the boat, someone suggested we drink amaretto sours. Amaretto sours are for sipping, for having one, maybe two, cocktails. We probably had many more than two that night and they were probably made from some kind of mix. Years later, when John said he was making amaretto sours, I winced. Thankfully, his proper amaretto sour has restored the reputation of this drink for me and I have been able to appreciate it at an appropriate sipping pace.

Makes 1 cocktail

Ice

1 ounce amaretto

1 ounce whiskey

1 ounce lemon juice

1 ounce half-sweet
    simple syrup

1 ounce soda water

Fancy cherries for garnish

HALF-SWEET SIMPLE SYRUP

1/2 cup sugar

1 cup water

1. To make the half-sweet simple syrup: In a small saucepan over medium heat, combine the sugar and water. Bring the mixture to a low boil. Stir until the sugar dissolves. Turn off the heat and let it cool completely. Store leftover syrup in a glass jar in the refrigerator for up to 3 weeks.

2. Fill a cocktail shaker with ice. Add the amaretto, whiskey, lemon juice, and half-sweet simple syrup. Put the lid on the shaker and shake for 30 seconds, until the ingredients are chilled.

3. Pour the cocktail into an ice-filled glass, straining it with the shaker. Add the soda water, stir, and garnish with a fancy cherry.

COFFEE CRÈME BRÛLÉE

At Spoons Bistro in Victor, Idaho, they used to serve a great crème brûlée. The thought of making it myself has always intimidated me, but after having it at Spoons, I decided to broaden my horizons. I'm so glad I did. These are great to make ahead for a fancy dinner party. No one needs to know how easy they are! You can also make it in one pie dish instead of ramekins, which makes it easier to sneak in a few bites from the fridge throughout the day. Mmmmm.

Makes 8 servings

4 cups heavy whipping cream

4 tablespoons coarsely ground espresso coffee beans

½ teaspoon ground cinnamon

1 teaspoon vanilla extract

1 cup plus 8 teaspoons sugar, divided

8 large egg yolks

1. Place 8 ramekin cups in a large roasting pan and set aside.

2. In a saucepan, combine the heavy cream, ground espresso beans, cinnamon, vanilla, and 1 cup of the sugar. Bring the mixture to a low boil, whisking until the sugar and espresso are combined.

3. Remove the saucepan from the heat. Cover the saucepan and let it stand for 30 minutes. After it has cooled, strain the liquid through a fine sieve.

4. Preheat the oven to 325 degrees. Bring a medium saucepan with water to a boil.

5. Using a stand mixer or hand mixer, whisk the egg yolks until they are frothy and light colored, about 2 minutes. Using a ladle, slowly whisk a little of the warm cream mixture into the eggs to temper them and keep the eggs from scrambling. Once the eggs have tempered, slowly add the rest of the cream mixture, whisking until combined. Skim or strain the foam off the top of the custard mixture before pouring it into the ramekins.

6. Divide the custard mixture into the ramekins in the pan. Then pour enough boiling water into the roasting pan to come halfway up the sides of the ramekins.

7. Bake until the center of the custard moves only slightly when the ramekins

HOT LITTLE TIP

Torch It!

If you have a kitchen torch, you can skip the broiling step. After the custards have chilled in the fridge, sprinkle the sugar on top and then use the torch to caramelize the sugar. A torch is not a *must-have* tool in my kitchen, but I do recommend it for the fun of it!

are gently shaken, about 35 to 45 minutes.

8. Carefully remove the ramekins from the pan and let the custard cool. Refrigerate uncovered for at least 3 hours or overnight.

9. Preheat the oven broiler to high heat.

10. Sprinkle 1 teaspoon of the sugar over each custard. Place the ramekins on a rimmed baking sheet. Broil the custards until the sugar is brown and caramelized, about 1 to 2 minutes, rotating the baking sheet halfway through to broil evenly. Watch closely to avoid burning. Chill for 1 hour before serving.

TRIPLE TREAT BROWNIES

This brownie recipe is the result of a fun project with the girls, during one of my attempts at Mom of the Year. I always wanted to be the mom who had cookies and brownies waiting for my children when they got home from school. I wouldn't say it's worked out exactly like that, but my daughters and I do spend many, many happy hours cooking together in the kitchen. When those hours are spent making a sweet treat, it's even more fun. This recipe is all about my love for baking with the girls . . . and my love of chocolate!

Makes 10 to 12 servings (24 2-inch brownies)

1 cup (2 sticks) plus
    1 tablespoon
    butter, divided
12 ounces semisweet
    chocolate chips
4 large eggs

2 cups sugar
2 teaspoons vanilla extract
1 ½ cups plus 3
    tablespoons cake
    flour (or 1 ½ cups
    all-purpose flour)

½ cup unsweetened cocoa
1 teaspoon baking powder
1 teaspoon salt
6 ounces dark
    chocolate chips

1. Preheat the oven to 350 degrees.
2. Use 1 tablespoon of the butter to grease a 9 x 13-inch glass or metal baking dish.
3. In a double boiler (or in the microwave) melt the semisweet chocolate chips and the remaining 1 cup of butter, stirring well to combine. Remove it from the heat and let it cool.
4. Once the chocolate mixture has cooled, gently whisk in the eggs, sugar, and vanilla.
5. In a large bowl, combine the flour, cocoa, baking powder, and salt and whisk.
6. Slowly add the dry ingredients to the chocolate mixture and stir until well combined.

Note: I prefer dark cocoa, but other types work well too.

7. Pour the batter into the buttered baking dish. Sprinkle the dark chocolate chips over the top.
8. Bake for 30 to 32 minutes, or until a toothpick inserted in the center comes out clean, turning the pan halfway through baking.

HOT LITTLE TIP

Cast Iron for a Crispy Brownie Crust

I like to use a cast-iron skillet for these brownies. Once the oven is preheated, I melt 1 tablespoon of the butter in the bottom of the skillet and then pour the batter on top. It makes the bottom of the brownies nice and crispy.

WINTER

In November and December, the Callie's production facility is a crazy symphony of busy biscuiteers, a wild blur that Santa's elves could relate to. It's always a puzzle to figure out how to fill every order, and each year we try to make and pack more than the year before. Each day is an all-hands-on-deck race, from six in the morning to as late as nine o'clock at night. Stacked boxes fill the wraparound porch and bust out the rear loading dock. FedEx visits several times a day for pickups. We eat standing up, and on occasion a massage therapist comes in for quick back rubs and hand massages, to give the biscuiteers a moment's relief and pampering.

We work hard going down our list of orders and making sure we don't miss anyone because customers tell us how our biscuits have become a tradition at their holiday parties, on Christmas morning, and to give as gifts. They are counting on us to deliver! We save our party for after the holidays, when we can really enjoy it and celebrate another wild season.

With all of this happy chaos, good food at home is more needed than ever to keep us going. I gravitate toward soups, stews, and braised meats. I look for ways to make hearty meals happen on busy school nights, when the sun sets early and practices go on past dark. The fireplace at our house stays very active this time of year. After a day of filling orders at the biscuit house and shuttling the girls to and from sports, what a pleasure it is to pour a glass of red wine, sidle up next to the fire, and sink into a place of gratitude and love for everyone working so hard at the facility, all the people who have made Callie's part of their holiday traditions, and my family, who inspires everything I do. What a beautiful season to eat and drink to all that's good and to celebrate all of our hard work with those we love.

WEEKNIGHT
SUPPERS

FRENCH ONION SOUP WITH GRUYÈRE BISCUIT CROUTONS

Cate can make this soup in her sleep! It's one of her personal favorites, and I'm so proud she can do it all on her own. This is a great recipe to start with when you're teaching children to cook. It uses mostly pantry staples, but it feels kinda fancy, especially with the cheesy crouton on top.

Makes 4 to 6 servings (48 ounces total)

2 tablespoons salted butter
1 white onion, sliced
    (about 2 cups)
1 red onion, sliced
    (about 2 cups)
2 large yellow onions,
    sliced (about 4 cups)
4 cloves garlic, minced
    (about 4 teaspoons)
2 teaspoons sugar
1 bay leaf

Salt and freshly ground
    coarse black
    pepper to taste
2 tablespoons all-
    purpose flour
1/2 cup dry red wine
5 sprigs fresh thyme,
    tied into a bundle
    with kitchen twine
1 quart beef stock (or
    vegetable stock)

Parmesan cheese rind
1/2 cup water
6 buttermilk biscuits
    (page 5)
1 cup grated Gruyère
    cheese
Chopped fresh flat-
    leaf Italian parsley
    for garnish

1. Heat a Dutch oven or large pot over medium heat. Add the butter.

2. Once the butter has melted, add the onions, garlic, sugar, bay leaf, and salt and pepper. Cook the onions for 40 to 45 minutes, or until well cooked and tender. They will be brown and caramelized.

3. Add the flour and stir to coat. Cook 3 to 5 minutes. Add the red wine and cook for another 5 minutes.

4. Add the thyme, beef stock, Parmesan rind, and water. Cook over medium-low heat for 30 minutes, stirring occasionally.

5. Meanwhile, preheat the oven broiler to high. Line a rimmed baking sheet with parchment paper.

6. Slice the biscuits in half and place them on the baking sheet. Top the biscuits with the Gruyère and broil for 2 to 3 minutes, or until the cheese has melted and crisped, watching carefully so the biscuits don't burn.

7. Serve the soup in bowls with the cheesy biscuits on top and garnished with the parsley.

HOT LITTLE TIP

Cooking the onions for 40 to 45 minutes may seem like a long time, but you want them to be dark, dark brown. Cook low and slow!

MEATBALL SUB SANDWICHES

I started making these subs when the girls were having volleyball and soccer practices that lasted as late as nine o'clock at night. I was determined to figure out a good, hearty meal I could pack in a container and take with me in the carpool line. These sandwiches actually get better wrapped up ahead of time, as the sauce soaks into the bread a little, so they're perfect anytime you need a warm sammie on the go.

Makes 4 sandwiches

TOMATO SAUCE

I tablespoon bacon grease
   (or other oil)
2 yellow onions, chopped
   (about I ½ cups)

4 cloves garlic, minced
   (about 4 teaspoons)
2 (28-ounce) cans or

boxes good-quality
   diced tomatoes
8 to 10 basil leaves,
   chopped, optional

MEATBALLS

½ pound ground pork
½ pound ground beef
½ pound ground lamb
3 cloves garlic, minced
½ white onion, minced

½ teaspoon crushed
   red pepper flakes
6 basil leaves, chopped
I large egg, lightly beaten
Salt and freshly ground

coarse black
   pepper to taste
I to 2 cups fresh bread
   crumbs, divided
2 tablespoons bacon
   grease (or other oil)

SANDWICHES

4 good-quality sub rolls

I cup baby spinach,
   stems removed

8 ounces fresh mozzarella,
   roughly chopped

1. To make the tomato sauce: Heat the bacon grease in a saucepan over medium heat. Add the onions and stir frequently until soft and golden brown, about 8 minutes. Add the garlic and sauté 60 to 90 seconds more, or until you can really smell the garlic. Add the tomatoes and basil (if using) and cook over medium heat, at a light simmer, for 45 minutes to I hour, stirring occasionally.

2. While the sauce is simmering, prepare the meatballs. Preheat the oven to 400 degrees.

3. In a large bowl, combine the pork, beef, lamb, garlic, onions, red pepper flakes, basil, egg, and salt and pepper. Add ½ cup of the bread crumbs and mix to combine.

4. Roll the mixture into 2- to 2 ½-tablespoon balls (about the size of

a golf ball). Roll each meatball in the remaining bread crumbs.

5. Heat a large cast-iron skillet (or other ovenproof skillet) over medium-high heat. Add the bacon grease to the skillet. Sear the meatballs in the skillet, making sure they are just lightly browned on each side.

6. Immediately move the pan to the oven and cook for 20 minutes, turning the meatballs after 10 minutes so they brown on all sides. Remove the skillet from the oven and let the meatballs rest for 5 to 10 minutes.

7. Preheat the oven broiler to high.

8. On each sub roll, place 3 meatballs, $1/4$ cup tomato sauce, $1/4$ cup baby spinach, and a fourth of the mozzarella cheese. Broil for 1 to 2 minutes, or until the cheese melts, watching carefully so the sandwiches don't burn.

Note: You can freeze any leftover meatballs.

HOT LITTLE TIP

No Soggy Subs

I wrap these subs up in parchment paper instead of foil, as foil tends to make them soggy. I use big sheets of the paper like they do in sub shops so that the girls can use them as catchalls in their laps. I also make sure to include a napkin or three inside the parchment wrap!

COCONUT SALMON

We eat a lot of salmon. It's healthy, it keeps well in the freezer, and it can make a meal in minutes. The coconut milk over rice in this recipe creates a beautiful gravy that for me brings to mind an Asian take on my Southern roots of rice and gravy. Comfort food in any language!

Makes 4 servings

1 tablespoon olive oil

2 tablespoons minced garlic

2 tablespoons minced fresh ginger

1 orange, red, or yellow bell pepper, diced (about 1 cup)

1 (13.5-ounce) can full-fat coconut milk

2 tablespoons fish sauce, divided

2 tablespoons soy sauce, divided

Juice and zest of 2 medium limes, divided (about 4 tablespoons juice and 2 teaspoons zest)

Nonstick cooking spray

1 pound salmon, cut into 4 pieces

Cooked white rice for serving

2 tablespoons chopped fresh mint for garnish

2 tablespoons chopped fresh cilantro for garnish

2 tablespoons chopped fresh basil for garnish

2 green onions, diced, for garnish

2 tablespoons cashews for garnish

1. Add the olive oil to a large sauté pan over medium heat. Add the garlic, ginger, and bell peppers and cook for 6 to 8 minutes, or until the peppers begin to soften.

2. Add the coconut milk, stirring to combine. Add 1 tablespoon of the fish sauce, 1 tablespoon of the soy sauce, 2 tablespoons of the lime juice, and all of the lime zest to the coconut milk. Let it simmer while you cook the salmon.

3. Preheat the oven broiler to high. Line a rimmed baking sheet with foil. Spray the foil with nonstick cooking spray.

4. In a medium bowl, combine the remaining fish sauce, soy sauce, and lime juice. Add the salmon to the bowl and toss it in the sauce.

5. Place the salmon on the foil-lined baking sheet and broil for approximately 3 to 5 minutes on each side for 1-inch thick fish, or until desired doneness. (I like mine medium rare.)

6. Place the salmon on the rice. Pour the coconut broth over the salmon and rice. Garnish with the fresh mint, cilantro, basil, green onions, and cashews to serve.

CAST-IRON CHICKEN ENCHILADAS

I have to thank my childhood friend Jennifer for introducing me to this recipe. It ticks all the boxes for the perfect winter weeknight supper: it's comforting, filling, and child and adult approved, with the convenience of a one-pot meal. You can prepare it ahead of time between the school shuffle and the sports shuffle, then pop it in the oven when you get home. In a pinch, you can even use a rotisserie chicken. If I'm making it ahead, I go through all the steps before baking, then I put foil over it and leave it on top of the stove until it's time to put it in the oven.

Makes 5 servings ♡ ☺

1 tablespoon olive oil

½ onion, chopped (about ½ cup)

1 green or red bell pepper, chopped (about 1 cup)

2 (4-ounce) cans green chilies

½ teaspoon cumin

½ teaspoon chili powder

½ teaspoon coriander

1 teaspoon salt

1 (8-ounce) package cream cheese

2 chicken breasts, fully cooked and shredded

Olive oil

1 cup freshly shredded cheese plus more for sprinkling (I like a

mix of sharp Cheddar and Monterey Jack)

5 large corn tortillas

½ cup heavy whipping cream or half-and-half

1 (10-ounce) can enchilada sauce (red or green)

½ bunch fresh cilantro, chopped

1. Preheat the oven to 375 degrees.
2. In a large skillet, heat the olive oil over medium heat. Add the onions and bell peppers and sauté until tender. Add the green chilies, cumin, chili powder, coriander, and salt. Stir to combine.
3. Mix in the cream cheese. Once it's well incorporated, add the shredded chicken and stir to combine.
4. Brush a cast-iron skillet with the olive oil and sprinkle a small amount of cheese on top. Warm the skillet over medium-low heat until the cheese begins to bubble.
5. Fill the tortillas one at a time with the chicken mixture, rolling each one like a burrito and then placing them side by side in the warm cast-iron skillet.
6. Sprinkle the shredded cheese on top of the enchiladas and pour the heavy cream or half-and-half over the top.
7. Put the cast-iron skillet in the oven and bake until golden and crispy, about 15 to 20 minutes.
8. Warm the enchilada sauce in a small saucepan to serve on the side. (Or you can pour the sauce over the enchiladas after baking and then return the skillet to the oven for 10 more minutes.)
9. Sprinkle the enchiladas with the cilantro. Serve with pico de gallo or Avocado Salsa (page 172), tortilla chips, and a crisp green salad.

CRISPY SHEPHERD'S PIE

I love shepherd's pie. I love lamb. I do not love mashed potatoes. They're just something I don't crave. They're a little too mushy for my texture-obsessed palate. So this is my idea of shepherd's pie with all the parts of it I love, along with the added crunch of crispy potatoes on top instead of mashed. It's a lighter spin on the traditional pie, which my whole family gobbles up.

Makes 6 to 8 servings

1 ½ pounds ground lamb (can substitute beef)

Salt and freshly ground coarse black pepper to taste

2 tablespoons butter, divided

1 cup frozen pearl onions

2 large carrots, peeled and chopped

¾ cup frozen peas

1 tablespoon all-purpose flour

½ cup beef broth

½ cup red wine

1 tablespoon tomato paste

½ teaspoon chopped fresh rosemary

1 teaspoon chopped fresh thyme

1 teaspoon chopped fresh flat-leaf Italian parsley plus more for garnish

Reserved grease from lamb

2 large Idaho or russet potatoes, peeled and sliced paper thin

½ cup freshly grated Parmesan cheese

1. Preheat the oven to 400 degrees.

2. Heat a cast-iron skillet (or other oven-proof skillet) over medium heat. Add the lamb and season with salt and pepper. Cook for 10 minutes, or until the meat is no longer pink, breaking the meat into smaller pieces as it cooks.

3. Drain the grease from the meat using a colander or strainer, reserving the grease, and set aside.

4. Add 1 tablespoon of the butter to the same skillet over medium heat. Add the onions and carrots. Sauté for 8 to 9 minutes. Add the peas and cook for another minute.

5. Add the flour to the skillet and stir until the vegetables are coated. Add the beef broth, red wine, tomato paste, and the remaining tablespoon of butter.

Stir until all is combined and the sauce thickens. Taste for salt and pepper.

6. Add the lamb back to the skillet. Stir in the rosemary, thyme, and parsley. If the mixture seems too dry, add some of the reserved grease. Add more salt and pepper if needed.

7. Layer a third of the sliced potatoes on top of the lamb mixture in the skillet. Sprinkle with a third of the Parmesan cheese and some salt and pepper. Repeat the layers two more times.

8. Bake in the oven for 30 minutes. Turn the oven to high broil and broil for 2 minutes, or until the potatoes are crisped, watching carefully so the potatoes don't burn.

9. Garnish with chopped parsley and serve immediately.

OKRA RICE

Okra and rice—two of my favorite things! My mom has made this dish for catered parties for years, and it's a staple at our house. You can eat it on its own or as a side. It's part of my routine of weeknight meals, but it's dinner party–worthy as well!

Makes 4 to 6 servings

I pound okra, ends trimmed and chopped

I ½ cups diced white onion, divided

¼ teaspoon cayenne

pepper (or more to taste)

½ teaspoon salt

¼ teaspoon freshly ground coarse black pepper

I to 3 tablespoons butter, divided

I to 2 tablespoons olive oil

2 cups cooked Basmati rice

1. In a medium bowl, combine the okra and ½ cup of the onions. Add the cayenne, salt, and black pepper. Let it sit for a few minutes for the flavors to meld.

2. In a cast-iron skillet over medium-high heat, melt I tablespoon of the butter. Add the okra mixture and spread in a single layer. Do not crowd the pan—you may need to cook in two batches. Let the okra cook undisturbed for 6 to 8 minutes.

3. Turn the okra to brown the other side, about 6 to 8 minutes more, leaving it undisturbed so it gets crispy. Once the okra is brown and crisp, remove it to a paper bag to drain the excess grease.

4. While the okra is draining, sauté the remaining cup of onions in the cast-iron skillet. Add oil if needed.

5. Preheat the oven to 350 degrees.

6. In a large bowl, combine the okra and onions with the cooked rice. Mix well and put it back into the cast-iron skillet.

7. Add I to 2 tablespoons of butter and additional pepper to taste. Bake until the butter melts and the rice is hot.

HOT LITTLE TIPS

The Art of Table Conversation . . . with Teenagers

With soccer practices, volleyball games, homework, and running a business, sometimes even my family's sit-down suppers at home feel like they're grab-and-go. Still, sitting down together for supper is a priority. It doesn't matter if it's a twenty-minute meal, something that took all day to make, or even takeout.

A lot of days, the dinner table is the only chance we get to really talk to each other. The art of conversation is an important lifelong skill. However, if you've ever sat at a table with children, especially teenagers, you know the conversation doesn't always . . . flow. Here are two of my favorite ways to get a good conversation going:

- TableTopics cards: These cards have icebreaker questions like, "What's the hardest thing you've ever done?" and "What would you like to be famous for?" that give us a starting point for conversation. Before long we're having a real conversation and sometimes asking hard questions. I love being surprised by what my children say! These cards come in several different versions, and you can even make your own cards: spend a supper conversation coming up with the questions together and write them down on cards to use later.

- Blessing vase: You don't need to wait for Thanksgiving for this one. I put an empty glass vase in the middle of the dinner table, and for a week the girls put strips of different-colored construction paper at each person's plate. When we sit down for supper, we write down something we were thankful for that day and take turns reading them out loud and then putting the strips in the vase. By the end of the week, we have a vase bursting with all the beautiful colors of our blessings. We're reminded in a visual way that even bad days can end on a brighter note when we take the time to sit down together.

Conversation and the togetherness that comes from sitting down together can comfort and heal the hurts of the day, and strengthen us for the next day. With all that on the line, our suppertime together doesn't have to be perfect—it just has to happen. And the same goes for our conversation.

It doesn't have to be the dazzling family discussion of my dreams to make a positive difference. I try to keep my expectations reasonable, and more often than not the tension melts, the comments start, and before we know it, we're sharing and laughing.

Start a conversation at your table and see where it goes! It might not be deep. It might go off the rails. It might make you cry. You never know down the line, in the years to come, what kind of impact having these regular dinner conversations will have, even if on the surface they aren't all that mind-blowing. In the short term, whether they go as planned or not, they're a break from all the craziness, when we get to show we're here for each other and that we care what's going on in each other's lives and what each of us has to say about it. Teenagers aren't always the most eager conversationalists, but with a little practice, they may surprise you!

WEEKEND
SUPPERS

ITALIAN WEDDING SOUP

It was a rare snow day. Everything was covered in white. There was no school, no cable TV, and no internet. The whole neighborhood was going a bit crazy. All the stores and restaurants were closed. I had to come up with something to cook from what we had in the fridge. "How about Italian wedding soup?" I suggested. The girls were all over that. *Wedding* soup? While I started the soup, they took the opportunity to plan an Italian wedding of their own. They made invitations and went around the neighborhood passing them out. They rearranged the furniture to make rows of chairs, with an aisle in the middle. They made programs. A neighbor mom and I dressed in "mother-of-the-bride" and "mother-of-the-groom" outfits. Other neighbors came wearing everything from pajamas to jeans to formal dresses. During the ceremony, Cate "got hitched" to a boy in the neighborhood, and then we all ate soup and had a champagne toast. Everyone left feeling full, with delicious soup in their bellies and the intoxication of fun and friendship in their hearts. One of my favorite wintertime memories!

Makes 4 to 6 servings (2 quarts total)   (W)

SOUP

2 tablespoons butter

3 to 4 celery stalks, finely chopped

4 carrots, finely chopped

1 large white onion, diced (about 1 cup)

5 cloves garlic, minced (about 5 teaspoons)

32 ounces chicken stock

3 cups water

Parmesan cheese rind

½ teaspoon crushed red pepper flakes

8 sprigs fresh thyme

5 sprigs fresh oregano

10 sprigs fresh flat-leaf Italian parsley

½ cup ditalini or orzo pasta

Salt and freshly ground coarse black pepper to taste

2 cups fresh spinach

Buttery garlic bread to serve

MEATBALLS

Nonstick cooking spray

1 pound ground pork

1 large egg

¼ cup bread crumbs

¼ cup finely grated Parmesan cheese

2 green onions, sliced

2 tablespoons minced fresh flat-leaf Italian parsley

Salt and freshly ground coarse black pepper to taste

1. In a large Dutch oven or pot, heat the butter over medium heat. Add the celery, carrots, and onions. Sauté until the vegetables have softened, about 3 to 5 minutes. Add the garlic and cook for another minute.

2. Add the chicken stock, water, Parmesan rind, and crushed red pepper. Tie

CERVEZA-SOAKED CARNITAS

This is a slow-cooker recipe, so when you finally make it home after all the day's activities, you get to walk into a house filled with a spicy-sweet aroma and a taco supper that's ready to go. As a bonus, the leftovers magically evolve from carnitas to a savory soup similar to posole. I love a dish that only gets better over time!

Makes 8 to 10 servings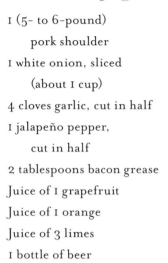

I (5- to 6-pound)
   pork shoulder
I white onion, sliced
   (about I cup)
4 cloves garlic, cut in half
I jalapeño pepper,
   cut in half
2 tablespoons bacon grease
Juice of I grapefruit
Juice of I orange
Juice of 3 limes
I bottle of beer

Warm corn tortillas
   for serving
Freshly chopped
   avocado for
   garnish
Pico de gallo for
   garnish
Cotija or feta cheese
   for garnish
Sliced limes for
   garnish
Sliced jalapeños
   for garnish

SPICE RUB

2 teaspoons cumin
I tablespoon chili powder
2 teaspoons dried oregano
I teaspoon ground
   cinnamon

$^1/_2$ teaspoon cayenne
   pepper
I tablespoon salt
Freshly ground coarse
   black pepper

> ### HOT LITTLE TIP
>
> #### Carnitas in a Bowl
>
> To make leftover carnitas into soup, in a pot or saucepan combine the leftover meat and any leftover juices with beef or chicken stock and whatever vegetables you have on hand. Let it simmer, then serve the soup by itself, over rice, or over grits. You'll be surprised by how much flavor this next-day creation packs!

1. To make the spice rub: In a small bowl, combine the cumin, chili powder, oregano, cinnamon, cayenne, salt, and pepper. Pat the dry rub all over the pork.

2. In a slow cooker, combine the onions, garlic, and jalapeño.

3. In a cast-iron skillet or Dutch oven, heat the bacon grease over medium-high heat. Carefully place the pork in the skillet and sear I to 2 minutes on all sides.

4. Remove the pork and place it in the slow cooker. Over the pork, pour the grapefruit juice, orange juice, lime juice, and beer. Cook in the slow cooker on the high setting for 4 to 5 hours or on the low setting for 8 to 9 hours, until

the meat is tender. Or you can bake it, covered, at 325 degrees for 3 to 3 ½ hours, until the meat is tender and easily shreds.

5. Preheat the oven broiler to high. Remove the pork from the slow cooker. Separate and discard the bone and fat.

Pull the meat apart and place it on a rimmed baking sheet. Broil it on the baking sheet for 5 minutes, or until the meat has crisped.

6. Serve with the warm tortillas and the avocado, pico de gallo, cheese, lime, and jalapeños.

PORK RAGU WITH PAPPARDELLE

When you serve this pasta to guests, they'll think you've been toiling away at it all day long! They don't need to know how easy it really is. It does take a few hours, but that's cooking time in the oven, not heavy lifting for the cook. This is Sarah's birthday supper request, the ultimate seal of approval in our house. Noodles lacquered in slow-roasted pork fat and au jus . . . need I say more?

Makes 6 servings

1 (3-pound) pork shoulder
Salt and freshly ground
    coarse black pepper
2 tablespoons canola oil
1 white onion, chopped
    (about 1 cup)
1 clove garlic, minced
    (about 1 teaspoon)
Zest and juice of 2
    lemons (about 4

teaspoons zest and 6
    tablespoons juice)
1 cup dry white wine
1 cup chicken stock
6 sprigs fresh thyme,
    tied in a bundle
    with kitchen twine
Parmesan cheese rind
3 large carrots, peeled and
    chopped into quarters
1 pound pappardelle

pasta (or black pepper
    pappardelle)
1 cup reserved pasta water
1 (10-ounce) bag
    fresh spinach
3 tablespoons butter
1/4 cup chopped fresh flat-
    leaf Italian parsley
1/4 cup freshly grated
    Parmesan cheese

1. Preheat the oven to 325 degrees.
2. Season both sides of the pork with salt and pepper. Heat a large Dutch oven over medium-high heat and add the canola oil.
3. Sear the pork on all sides, about 3 to 4 minutes per side. Remove the pork from the pot and set it aside on a plate. Reduce the heat to medium low. Add the onions and garlic and sauté for 2 to 3 minutes, scraping up all of the brown bits stuck to the bottom.
4. Add the pork back to the pot with the onions and garlic. Add the lemon zest and juice, wine, stock, thyme bundle, and Parmesan rind. Put the lid on the pot and cook in the oven for 1 hour, then turn the pork and cook another hour.
5. After the additional hour, add the

carrots and stir them in. Cook in the oven for 20 to 30 minutes.
6. Remove the thyme bundle and Parmesan rind. With two forks, pull off the fatty parts of the pork while separating the meat into shreds. Discard the fatty pieces.
7. Boil the pasta in salted water and cook according to the directions on the box for al dente. Before you drain the pasta, reserve one cup of the pasta water and set aside.
8. Add the pasta, spinach, and butter to the shredded pork in the Dutch oven. Stir to combine. Turn the stove top to low heat to incorporate the ingredients. Add a little of the pasta water to thicken the mixture.
9. Remove from the heat and top with the parsley and grated Parmesan to serve.

HOT LITTLE TIP

Even More Special with Morels

Want to take this ragu over the top? Add some morel mushrooms. My nephew Sam forages for morels in the mountains in Idaho, and sometimes he comes home with more than we could possibly eat—which provides an ideal excuse to make this ragu. Sauté fresh morels in butter, then add them to the Dutch oven with the pork at the same time as the lemon zest and juice, wine, stock, thyme, and Parmesan rind. If you buy morels at the grocery store and they are dried, not fresh, simply rehydrate them before adding them to the pot. To rehydrate, place the morels in a bowl or shallow dish, cover them with water, stock, or wine, and let them sit for about 20 minutes. Then drain the morels and add them to the pot.

COWBOY BEANS

My mother-in-law makes this dish every Fourth of July as a side to steak. It's so much more delicious than what you think of when you think of "beans." I cooked up my version for the Charleston Wine + Food festival to make Frito Pie. We put Fritos in parchment bags, poured on the beans, and topped them off with some of my favorite accoutrements! I've served it at several parties since then, and it's been a surefire hit every time.

Makes 6 to 8 servings

1 (16-ounce) bag
    pinto beans
2 tablespoons butter
2 tablespoons olive oil
4 cloves garlic, minced
    (about 4 teaspoons)
1/2 white onion, chopped
    (about 1/2 cup)
2 celery stalks, chopped
    (about 1 cup)
1/2 cup chopped carrots
    (about 1 large carrot)

1 green bell pepper,
    chopped (about 1 cup)
1 (1 1/2-pound) pork jowl
1 quart chicken stock
12 stems fresh thyme,
    tied into a bundle
    with kitchen twine
12 stems fresh flat-leaf
    Italian parsley, tied
    into a bundle with
    kitchen twine
2 teaspoons cumin

2 teaspoons chili powder
2 teaspoons coriander
1 bay leaf
Fritos
Pimento cheese
Sour cream
Schug (page 221)
Radish slices
Fresh cilantro

1. Rinse the pinto beans and soak them overnight.
2. In a 5-quart Dutch oven, heat the butter and olive oil over medium heat. Add the garlic, onions, celery, carrots, and bell peppers and sauté until tender.
3. Add the soaked beans and their liquid.
4. Add the pork jowl and bring it to a boil.
5. Add the chicken stock, thyme bundle, parsley bundle, cumin, chili powder, coriander, and bay leaf. Reduce the heat to a simmer and preheat the oven to 300 degrees.
6. Bake, covered, for 3 hours, until the beans are tender and the jowl meat shreds. Uncover and cook for 45 minutes. Remove the bay leaf. Remove the pork jowl and shred the meat. Return the meat to the beans.
7. Serve over Fritos with pimento cheese, sour cream, Schug, radishes, and cilantro for topping.

HOT

LITTLE

EXTRAS

SCHUG

This sauce—also spelled *zhug*, *zhoug*, *s'chug*, and *shough*—is a spicy green condiment first created by Yemeni Jews that made its way across the Middle East—and eventually to Charleston. Michael Shemtov of Charleston's Butcher & Bee turned me on to it served as a dollop on top of hummus. It's been fascinating my taste buds and imagination ever since! It has so many jalapeños in it that at first I couldn't figure out how it could ever work. But it does! Make some and keep it in your fridge to add as an accoutrement to Cowboy Beans, Veggie Tortilla Soup, nachos, steak, fish, grilled veggies, potatoes, fried eggs, even mixed into a vinaigrette or mayonnaise.

Makes 3 1/2 cups

10 jalapeño peppers, 8 with seeds and ribs removed and 2 with seeds and ribs intact for extra heat

10 cloves garlic

2 cups fresh cilantro leaves

2 cups fresh flat-leaf Italian parsley

1 tablespoon cumin

1 tablespoon coriander

1/2 teaspoon ground cardamom

Zest and juice of 1 lemon (about 2 teaspoons zest and 2 tablespoons juice)

1 to 2 teaspoons salt

3/4 to 1 cup olive oil

1. In a food processor fitted with a steel blade, combine the jalapeños and garlic and pulse.
2. Add the cilantro and parsley and pulse until a thick paste forms.
3. Add the cumin, coriander, cardamom, lemon zest and juice, and salt. Pulse to combine.

Note: Schug lasts for weeks in the fridge and also can be frozen.

4. Add about 1/2 cup of the olive oil. Blend well and salt to taste.
5. Slowly add the remaining olive oil to form a pesto-like sauce.

HOT LITTLE TIP

How Do You Like Your Heat?

Most of the jalapeño heat comes from the seeds and ribs, so you can play with the degree of spiciness by changing up how many intact peppers you use and how many you use without the seeds and ribs. You can also add plain yogurt to turn down the heat if you went a little overboard.

BAKED BRIE

I always keep a few jars of special preserves or jams on hand, and this recipe is a beautiful way to show them off. I recommend my Raspberry Pepper Preserves, but the Brie also works well with mint pepper jelly. As usual, I like a little spice to go with the sweet! Another way you can switch up the presentation is to bake it in a cast-iron skillet instead of on a baking sheet. Then serve it straight from the skillet—a little bit elegant, a little bit rustic.

Makes 6 to 8 servings

1 (8-ounce) wheel of Brie
1/2 cup favorite jam
   or preserves

1/2 cup roughly
   chopped pecans
Your favorite crackers

for serving

1. Preheat the oven to 350 degrees. Line a rimmed baking sheet with parchment paper.

2. Place the Brie on the parchment-lined baking sheet and bake for 20 minutes.

3. While the Brie is baking, in a small bowl combine the preserves and chopped pecans.

4. Remove the Brie from the oven and top with the preserves and pecans. Bake for another 5 minutes.

5. Remove the Brie from the oven and carefully transfer it to a serving dish. Serve immediately with crackers.

Note: I recommend using Callie's Hot Little Biscuit Raspberry Pepper Preserves for the jam in this recipe. Also, I prefer Callie's Hot Little Biscuit Cocktail Pecans, which are especially salty and buttery.

ROASTED BROCCOLINI AND WHITE BEANS

Never ever have I said, "I can't wait to eat more broccoli." This broccolini, however, is another story. It looks, smells, and tastes better than broccoli. It makes a super-delicious side for seared steak or salmon, and it's an easy way to get kids to eat their greens. It's simply easier and tastier to deal with in every way. I'm sorry, broccoli, but it's true!

Makes 4 to 6 servings

2 bunches broccolini
(about 1 pound)

½ small onion, sliced
(about ½ cup)

2 cloves garlic, minced
(about 2 teaspoons)

Zest and juice of 1 lemon,
divided (about 2

teaspoons zest and 2
tablespoons juice)

¼ teaspoon crushed
red pepper flakes

4 tablespoons olive oil

Salt and freshly ground
coarse black
pepper to taste

1 (15.5-ounce) can white
beans, rinsed and
drained (cannellini
beans preferred)

¼ cup pine nuts, toasted

3 tablespoons freshly
grated Parmesan
cheese

1. Preheat the oven to 400 degrees. Line a rimmed baking sheet with parchment paper.

2. In a large bowl, combine the broccolini, onions, garlic, lemon juice, red pepper flakes, olive oil, and salt and pepper and toss. Pour the mixture onto the parchment-lined baking sheet.

3. Bake for 10 minutes. Remove from the oven and add the beans. Bake for another 5 minutes.

4. Top with the lemon zest, pine nuts, and Parmesan and serve immediately.

TWICE-BAKED CAULIFLOWER PEPPERS

My girls love, I mean *love*, twice-baked potatoes. I don't even like to talk about twice-baked potatoes, and you can guess why. It's the mashed potato part. Too mushy for me! One of my favorite creative challenges is to take a dish the girls love and find a way to make it in a different form. With the cauliflower replacing the mashed potatoes and bright red peppers replacing the potato skins, this Keto-friendly alternative is healthier and, in my opinion, way better tasting than twice-baked you-know-whats!

Makes 5 servings

2 heads cauliflower, washed and cut into pieces (about 1 1/2 to 2 pounds florets)

1 white onion, diced (about 1 cup)

3 cloves garlic, peeled and smashed

3 tablespoons olive oil
Salt and freshly ground coarse black pepper to taste

5 large red bell peppers of similar size

4 tablespoons butter

3/4 cup heavy whipping cream

2 1/2 cups freshly shredded sharp Cheddar cheese, divided

Minced chives for garnish

Crumbled bacon for garnish, optional

1. Preheat the oven to 375 degrees. Line a rimmed baking sheet with parchment paper.

2. Place the cauliflower, onions, and garlic on the parchment-lined baking sheet. Drizzle with olive oil and salt and pepper to taste.

3. Bake for 40 minutes, or until the cauliflower is tender.

4. While the cauliflower is roasting, prepare the peppers. Cut off the tops and cut the peppers in half lengthwise and clean out the seeds.

5. Once the cauliflower is tender, remove it from the oven and reduce the temperature to 350 degrees.

6. In a large Dutch oven, melt the butter over medium heat.

7. Add the roasted cauliflower, onions,

and garlic to the Dutch oven, stirring to coat. Remove the Dutch oven from the heat. Add the heavy cream and 2 cups of the cheese, stirring until combined. Add salt and pepper if needed.

8. Using an immersion blender or transferring it to a regular blender, blend the mixture to a rough texture. Do not overmix or the mixture will become watery.

9. Scoop the mixture into the pepper halves. Top each with the remaining 1/2 cup of cheese.

10. Place the peppers in the oven and bake for 15 minutes. Then turn the broiler to high and broil for 3 to 5 minutes, or until bubbly.

11. Garnish with chives and bacon, if using, to serve.

MAMA'S CABBAGE

This delicious, savory dish is a nostalgic memory for me of my grandmother Mama. She had many mouths to feed, and she knew how to make the most out of very little. She would serve this simple dish alongside fried pork chops, country-fried steak, or, most often, hamburger steak. This comfort dish warms my body and spirit.

Makes 4 to 6 servings

4 slices bacon

1 onion, diced
   (about 1 cup)

1 head green cabbage,

sliced very thinly
   (about 2 pounds)

Salt and freshly ground

coarse black
   pepper to taste

1/2 lemon (or more to taste)

Tabasco to taste

1. In a cast-iron skillet or sauté pan, cook the bacon until crispy. Remove the bacon from the skillet and let it drain on paper towels. Leave the bacon grease in the skillet. Crumble the bacon once it has cooled.

2. Add the onions to the skillet with the bacon grease. Cook the onions for about 5 minutes, or until the onions are soft and translucent.

3. Add the cabbage and the crumbled bacon.

4. Cook over medium heat, stirring occasionally, for about 20 minutes, or until the cabbage is tender.

5. Add salt and pepper to taste. Squeeze the lemon over the cabbage and add a couple dashes of Tabasco. Taste for lemon and spice and adjust to your taste. Stir to combine and serve immediately.

DRINKS
AND
DESSERTS

HOT CHOCOLATE

We started making hot chocolate at Callie's Hot Little Biscuit as a wintertime alternative to coffee, and it was an immediate success. Really, who doesn't love hot chocolate with a dollop of whipped cream on top?

Makes 20 tablespoons of mix; 10 total servings

½ cup sugar

½ cup cocoa

1 tablespoon cornstarch

1 ½ ounces semisweet chocolate, roughly chopped

1 ½ ounces bittersweet chocolate, roughly chopped

¼ teaspoon salt

Milk (16 ounces per serving)

Vanilla (¼ teaspoon per serving)

Whipped cream for garnish

Shaved chocolate for garnish

1. In a small bowl, combine the sugar, cocoa, cornstarch, semisweet chocolate, bittersweet chocolate, and salt.

2. In a saucepan, warm the milk and stir in the vanilla.

3. Stir in the dry mix (2 tablespoons per serving).

4. Transfer to a mug and top with whipped cream and shaved chocolate.

HOT LITTLE TIPS

Hot Chocolate for a Crowd

Come bearing a pot of warm, chocolatey goodness and be the hero of every wintertime event! Fill a 4-quart slow cooker with milk and set it to high heat. Once the milk is warm, add ½ cup of the dry mixture and 1 teaspoon of vanilla. The longer you let it sit, the better it tastes!

Mix Now, Make Later

Never buy those little paper packets of instant hot chocolate again! Make a big batch of the dry mix and divide it into mason jars to keep in your pantry for whenever you get the craving for a warm cup of chocolate cheer. Or spread some cheer—put a cute ribbon and a tag with instructions on the jars of mix and give them as gifts!

JOHN'S EGGNOG

John makes this eggnog every year for our Christmas Eve party. He ladles it from a massive serving bowl. The next morning, our Christmas tradition is to add a splash of the leftovers to our coffee. It takes the bite off the party from the night before, a little early-morning hair of the reindeer to help us get back into the holiday cheer. It's not a rare thing to see a neighbor amble over in a bathrobe and slippers with their coffee mug extended for their own little splash of John's holiday elixir!

Makes 12 to 14 servings

12 large eggs, yolks and whites separated
$\frac{1}{2}$ teaspoon vanilla extract
$\frac{1}{4}$ teaspoon ground cinnamon

$\frac{1}{4}$ teaspoon allspice
$\frac{1}{4}$ teaspoon salt
1 cup sugar, divided
1 cup whole milk

1 cup heavy whipping cream
1 cup bourbon
1 cup rum

1. In a large bowl, combine the egg yolks, vanilla, cinnamon, allspice, salt, and $\frac{1}{2}$ cup of the sugar. Whisk together.

2. In a medium bowl, using a stand mixer or hand mixer, beat the egg whites on medium-high speed while gradually adding the remaining $\frac{1}{2}$ cup of sugar. Continue to beat until stiff peaks form—this will take a couple of minutes.

3. Gently fold the egg white mixture into the egg yolk mixture until combined.

4. Slowly add the milk, heavy cream, bourbon, and rum. Stir until well combined.

5. Chill and stir the eggnog again before serving.

CRANBERRY AND APPLE CRISP WITH BISCUIT CRUMBLE

This crisp is perfect for putting in the oven while you're spending an afternoon decorating or wrapping presents. It smells like the holidays as it bakes, filling the house with a buttery, cinnamon aroma. Pull it out and serve it straight from the skillet, topped with ice cream. A delicious reward for all your merry work!

Makes 6 to 8 servings

- 2 tablespoons butter, divided
- 2 pounds apples, cored and peeled
- I cup fresh cranberries (can use frozen)
- 1/2 cup orange juice
- I tablespoon firmly packed brown sugar
- I tablespoon white sugar
- I teaspoon ground cinnamon
- I teaspoon vanilla extract
- Vanilla ice cream to serve

MAMA'S BUTTER PIECRUST

- 2 1/4 cups cake flour (or 2 cups all-purpose flour)
- 1/3 teaspoon kosher salt
- 12 tablespoons cold butter, cut into small cubes
- 5 to 7 tablespoons ice water

BISCUIT CRUMBLE TOPPING

- 3 leftover buttermilk biscuits, crumbled
- 1/4 cup pecans, crushed
- I tablespoon firmly packed brown sugar
- 1/2 teaspoon ground cinnamon
- 3 tablespoons butter

1. To make the piecrust: In a large bowl, combine the flour and the salt. Incorporate the butter into the flour, working the dough between your thumb and middle and pointer fingers to "snap" the dough together until the mixture resembles cottage cheese. It will be chunky, with some loose flour. Mix the cold water into the dough by the tablespoon, working it into the dough with your fingers until the dough holds together in a rough ball. Flour a sheet of waxed paper or parchment paper. Dump the dough onto the paper, sprinkle flour on the dough, and cover it with another sheet of parchment paper. Place the whole dough "sandwich" on a rimmed baking sheet and refrigerate 2 hours or overnight. Remove the dough from the fridge and let it sit out for 30 minutes still sandwiched in the paper.

2. To make the biscuit crumble topping: In a small bowl, combine the crumbled biscuits, crushed pecans, brown sugar, cinnamon, and butter. Incorporate with

your fingers until the mixture comes together in pea-size crumbs.

3. Preheat the oven to 350 degrees.

4. Melt 1 tablespoon of the butter in a 10-inch cast-iron skillet. Set it aside to cool.

5. In a large bowl, combine the apples, cranberries, orange juice, brown sugar, white sugar, cinnamon, and vanilla. Let it sit for 30 minutes.

6. With the piecrust dough still between the sheets of paper, roll it out into a 13-inch round and place it in the skillet. (Or you can make a free-form tart on a rimmed baking sheet.)

7. Pour the apple and cranberry mixture onto the crust, leaving enough space around the edges to fold the dough up and over the apples by $\frac{1}{2}$ to 1 inch.

8. Sprinkle the biscuit crumble topping over the apples and cranberries. Fold the dough up and over the apples for a rustic look, pleating as necessary.

9. Melt the remaining 1 tablespoon butter and brush it over the exposed dough. Bake for 50 to 60 minutes, or until the apples and cranberries are tender and the biscuit crumble topping and pastry are all browned.

10. Serve warm with vanilla ice cream or at room temperature.

Note: You can substitute store-bought crust for homemade. And I prefer Callie's Hot Little Biscuit Cocktail Pecans, which are especially salty and buttery.

CHOCOLATE CAKE

This recipe is the grand finale of this book, and I mean *grand*. It's a holiday, New Year's, birthday, or any day you really need a chocolate fix showstopper. It comes from my mom's best friends Sheryl and Bennett, who for years made this cake at their beloved Atlanta bakery, The Dessert Place. My mother makes it with my girls. It is over-the-top delicious and worth every calorie. I serve it at Christmas supper. It's a celebratory way to end one year and start another, and I think a perfect way to end this book. It feeds family and friends. It brings us together at the table to share its sweet richness. That's what my hot little suppers are all about: sharing the goodness in food and in each other, showing love, and feeling full.

HOT LITTLE TIP

Secret Substitute

Part of the fun of this chocolate cake for me is making it with the girls and, of course, getting to lick the batter and frosting, but I must confess: I have a secret source for when I run out of time and can't make it myself. Chocolate Cake Charleston makes (and ships!) an incredible chocolate cake. If you've got the craving but not the holiday bandwidth to make this cake happen in your own kitchen, outsource without shame. Everyone will love your substitute—it's up to you whether you tell them you didn't make it yourself!

Makes 8 to 10 servings

3/4 cup (1 1/2 sticks) butter, room temperature

2 1/4 cups firmly packed light brown sugar

3 large eggs, room temperature

3 ounces unsweetened chocolate, melted and slightly cooled

2 teaspoons vanilla extract

2 cups cake flour

2 teaspoons baking soda

3/4 teaspoon salt

1/2 cup buttermilk, room temperature

1 cup boiling water

FROSTING

1/2 cup (1 stick) unsalted butter, room temperature

1 tablespoon vegetable shortening

2 cups powdered sugar

1/4 cup chocolate syrup

3 ounces unsweetened chocolate, melted and slightly cooled

1/2 teaspoon salt

1 large egg yolk

2 teaspoons hot coffee

2 teaspoons vanilla extract

1. Preheat the oven to 350 degrees. Grease and flour two 8-inch round cake pans.

2. In a medium bowl, using an electric mixer, beat the butter on medium speed for 1 minute. Add the brown sugar and continue to beat on medium speed. Add the eggs one at a time. Beat until the mixture is light and fluffy, about 5 minutes.

3. Add the melted chocolate and vanilla. Mix until combined. Scrape down the sides of the bowl with a rubber spatula to make sure the ingredients are well blended.

4. In another medium bowl, combine the flour, baking soda, and salt. Add the dry ingredients to the chocolate batter a little at a time, alternating with the buttermilk. With the mixer on low speed, slowly add the boiling water. Once again, scrape down the sides of the bowl and mix well.

5. Pour the batter evenly into the prepared cake pans. Knock the pans on the counter several times to make sure the batter is evenly distributed and air bubbles are eliminated.

6. Bake on the center oven rack for 35

to 40 minutes, or until a toothpick inserted in the center comes out clean. Let the cakes cool on a wire rack for 20 minutes before removing them from the pans. Then let the cakes cool completely before frosting.

7. While the cakes are cooling, make the frosting. Using an electric mixer on medium speed, cream together the butter and shortening. Add half of the powdered sugar and scrape down the sides of the bowl with a rubber spatula. Mix in the chocolate syrup, melted chocolate, salt, and the remaining powdered sugar.

8. In a small bowl, combine the egg yolk, coffee, and vanilla and stir. Add the mixture to the frosting. Scrape down the sides of the bowl and mix on high for 2 minutes, or until the frosting is light and fluffy.

9. Put a little of the frosting on the cooled cakes, then put them in the freezer for 20 to 30 minutes to create a crumb coat.

10. Remove the cakes from the freezer, put frosting on top of one, top with the other cake, and frost all over.

Note: If you like a lot of frosting, double the frosting recipe.

ACKNOWLEDGMENTS

First, I thank my husband, John, and my girls, Caroline, Cate, and Sarah, for being my inspiration. I love that you always give me purpose and a reason to cook. The best part of my day every day is sitting around the table with you. That time grounds us, makes us stronger, and creates unforgettable memories as a family. Girls, you are such a gift to us, and I am so proud of the young ladies you've become. One day you will have your own families and be able to pass down all our traditions around your own supper tables. Never in my wildest dreams did I think I'd be able to balance being your mama with running multiple businesses and writing cookbooks. I could not have done any of it without you. Thank you for being the reason behind the whole journey. John, I have never-ending love and appreciation for you. Your love and support to keep me pursuing my dreams is everything. Thank you.

Thank you to my parents, Donald and Callie, and my extended parents, Caroline and Tom and Bees and Poppa. You have instilled in us the importance of family and helped us understand this is all that really matters in life! The tradition of sitting around the table is ever present in all of y'all, and I hope to continue what you have taught us by your example.

ABK, KCH, MBW, ABW, BLR, and KMD, I am proud to have such incredible friends in you. I appreciate your friendship and support, and I look forward to many more years of celebrating life together and many more margaritas along the way. Thank you for letting me cook for you, and thank you for all your physical and mental help with this little biscuit dream!

Amy Hughes, thank you for seeing something in me I still don't see in myself! You are a phenomenal agent and businessperson and, on top of that, a great friend and person. I appreciate all your love and confidence in me.

Libba Osborne, if you had told me fifteen years ago that we would still be in this biscuit game, I would have said no way! Throughout it all, you have been there for me. You make me look and sound way better than I could ever do on my own. I don't know how many times a week I say, "Let's ask Libba!" Thank you for keeping me in line and being such an incredible publicist and friend.

I can't thank my Callie's Hot Little Biscuit staff—my second family—enough. I am so lucky to be surrounded by such an amazing team of hardworking people. Thank you for being such an important part of this adventure with me, as we grow and continue to evolve together. I'm just the idea person, and you are the ones who make all our dreams come true. Thanks to all the "Biscuiteers" for all your hard work, energy, and good vibes. You inspire me and hold me accountable!

A special thanks to Tarah Boyleston, who has gone above wearing her marketing hat to bring this book's cover and the creative design aspect of the book to life! You go all-in and then some, and I truly appreciate your incredible work ethic and attention to detail!

Thanks also to Lindsay Narcisso, recipe tester and photographer for the Hot Little Suppers blog. Thank you for all your amazing testing and gorgeous photography. I can't make a recipe come to life from my brain to paper without you!

The Harper Horizon team has been wonderful and refreshing to work with. Andrea Fleck-Nisbet, thank you for the opportunity to bring this book into the world. I feel like we've had so much synergy from the very beginning, and I have thoroughly enjoyed the process. You are such a pleasure to work with.

Thank you, Amanda Bauch, for your tireless work on this book. Your positive energy, insightful comments, sense of humor, and impeccable attention to detail have made every aspect of this book better.

John Andrade, thank you for all of your planning and strategizing to get this cookbook in the hands of biscuit lovers everywhere!

To my writer, Bessie Gantt, it's so cool for someone who has no business writing a book to be paired up with someone like you. You get me and know what I'm going to say before I say it. I'm grateful to you for taking all my misspelled texts and emails and our hours of phone conversation and weaving it all together.

Angie Mosier, I feel honored to have you as the photographer for this book. You are so talented, not to mention enjoyable to work with and fun to be around. Photography is such an important aspect of a cookbook, and you make every dish, every location, every person look amazing. Thank you for your talents and your presence.

To my phenomenal recipe tester, Deidre Schipani, I am so grateful for the food knowledge and expertise you contributed to the book. I'm not a classically trained chef—I just love to cook. I appreciate that I get to share my recipes with you, and you make them better. I have learned much from you, and you have been a valuable part of this team.

My mentor, Nathalie Dupree, you are such a strong force in my life and career. You push me forward and give me the confidence to do things I didn't know I was capable of. You are such a positive person. Thank you for supporting me and so many other women in pursuing our culinary and business hopes and dreams. I hope to follow in your footsteps and help other women the way you have helped me.

Finally, to my Callie's Hot Little Biscuit family, fans, and customers. I am blown away and overwhelmed by your enthusiasm and support. Here we are with a second cookbook, opening four Callie's Hot Little Biscuit locations, and broadcasting a national PBS docuseries called *How She Rolls*, all about this journey. If it weren't for you, none of this could ever happen. I am grateful for your business and your encouragement. Your support allows me to raise my girls while doing something I absolutely love. Thank you for giving me the opportunity to be a tiny part of what you serve at your family supper table. That is a sacred responsibility I take very seriously. I am so honored!

APPENDIX A

Go-To Sides and Salad Dressings for Any Season

For a simple side dish that's not a big production, I sear, roast, or grill veggies at the last minute as the rest of the meal is coming together. For less delicate veggies, like broccoli and corn, I blanch them first in boiling water, then sear, roast, or grill to get some char on them.

Use whatever method is most convenient for you! If you are grilling the rest of the meal, blanch and then finish the veggies on the grill. If your oven is already hot from what you've been cooking, stick them in a 400-degree oven after tossing them in a little olive oil and salt and pepper. Then finish with lemon juice and zest or a quick Microplane swipe of Parmesan or pecorino cheese. And searing on the stove top in a cast-iron skillet that's smoking hot is always a winner.

Seared Veggies in Cast Iron (snow peas, snap peas, green beans, asparagus)

As the rest of your meal is finishing cooking, heat a cast-iron skillet on the stove until it's smoking hot. Toss the veggies in olive oil and salt and pepper, then sear them in the skillet just until they get a little color on them. Snow and snap peas take as little as a minute per side. Asparagus might take 4 to 6 minutes—thicker asparagus will take longer. Finish with salt and pepper. You can also add a splash of Dijon Mustard Vinaigrette. For an Asian flair, use peanut or toasted sesame oil instead of olive oil and finish with a splash of rice wine vinegar, lime juice or zest, and soy sauce.

Blanched and Seared Veggies (corn, broccoli, any veggie)

Place veggies in boiling water and blanch for 1 to 4 minutes, depending on the veggie. For corn, I boil for 4 minutes, turning after 2 minutes so it cooks evenly. For broccoli, boil a little less, especially if it's only florets. After boiling, dump the veggies in a colander and cover them with ice to stop them from cooking. Once they're cool, dry them off and finish them on the stove, searing as described above.

Versatile Salad Dressing with Variations for Any Green Salad

This is my go-to vinaigrette. I can make it with my eyes closed! As it is, it goes with almost any kind of green salad, but easy additions and substitutions can take it any direction based on your mood, theme, or what ingredients you have on hand.

DIJON MUSTARD VINAIGRETTE

Makes about 1 ½ cups

1 tablespoon Dijon mustard

1 clove garlic, minced

1 tablespoon minced onion (white, yellow, red, or green)

3/4 teaspoon honey

1 teaspoon lemon zest

1/4 cup sherry vinegar

(or champagne vinegar, white wine vinegar, or red wine vinegar)

1 cup extra-virgin olive oil

1/2 teaspoon salt

Freshly ground coarse black pepper

In a small bowl, combine the mustard, garlic, onions, honey, lemon zest, and vinegar. Whisk in the olive oil in a steady stream and add the salt and pepper to taste. Store in a mason jar and shake to blend before using.

HOT LITTLE TIP

Hot Little Shallot

I love to put half a shallot in a foil pouch drizzled with olive oil and salt and pepper and roast it for 30 minutes in a 350-degree oven. Then I use it in this vinaigrette in place of the garlic. So yummy . . . and makes your kitchen smell amazing!

FOR AN ASIAN TWIST TRY ANY OR ALL OF THE FOLLOWING:

Lime zest instead of lemon zest

Rice wine vinegar instead of sherry vinegar

Toasted sesame oil instead of olive oil

A drop of fish sauce

A drop or two of soy sauce

FOR A MEXICAN TWIST TRY ANY OR ALL OF THE FOLLOWING:

Lime zest instead of lemon zest

Cumin

Chopped fresh cilantro

OTHER ADDITIONS AND SUBSTITUTIONS TO TRY:

Balsamic vinegar

White balsamic vinegar

Chopped fresh flat-leaf Italian parsley or other chopped fresh herbs

Minced shallot

APPENDIX B

Resources

Callie's Hot Little Biscuit: calliesbiscuits.com

White Lily Self-Rising Flour: whitelily.com

Back in the Day Bakery: backinthedaybakery.com

Abundant Seafood: abundantseafood.co

Charleston Rice Steamer, Royall Ace Hardware: royallhardware.com

The Ordinary: eattheordinary.com

Tarvin Seafood, Inc.: misspaulashrimp.com

Ooni Pizza Ovens: ooni.com

Big Green Egg: biggreenegg.com

FIG: eatatfig.com

Café Altro Paradiso: altroparadiso.com

Rosa Mexicano: rosamexicano.com

Callie's Hot Little Biscuit Cocktail Pecans: calliesbiscuits.com

Hogwash Rose: store.hogwashrose.com

Graduate Columbia Hotel: graduatehotels.com/columbia

Callie's Hot Little Biscuit Fiery Pimento Cheese: calliesbiscuits.com

TableTopics Cards: tabletopics.com

Butcher & Bee: butcherandbee.com

Callie's Hot Little Biscuit Raspberry Pepper Preserves:
    calliesbiscuits.com (and for jellies, preserves, and relishes we
    don't carry, I turn to Mrs. Sassard's at sassards.com)

Chocolate Cake Charleston: chocolatecakecharleston.com

INDEX

ABOUT THE AUTHOR

Award-winning Southern food entrepreneur and mother of three, Carrie Morey is the founder and owner of Callie's Hot Little Biscuit and featured personality on *How She Rolls*, a documentary television series following Carrie on her whirlwind baking, business, and family adventures. She has grown her business from a small mail-order operation inspired by her mother's made-by-hand biscuits into a nationally recognized brand with a loyal following of biscuit-loving fans. She is the author of *Callie's Biscuits and Southern Traditions* and has appeared on *Today*, *The Martha Stewart Show*, and Food Network and been featured in *Saveur*, *Food & Wine*, *Southern Living*, *O the Oprah Magazine*, and the *New York Times*. She is a consultant for artisan food entrepreneurs, mentor at the University of South Carolina Darla Moore School of Business, and guest lecturer on entrepreneurship at the College of Charleston School of Business. She lives in Charleston, South Carolina, with her husband, John, and daughters, Caroline, Cate, and Sarah.